Workplace by Design

Franklin Becker / Fritz Steele

Workplace by Design

*Mapping the
High-Performance
Workscape*

Jossey-Bass Publishers • San Francisco

Substantial discounts on bulk quantities of Jossey-Bass books are available to corporations, professional associations, and other organizations. For details and discount information, contact the special sales department at Jossey-Bass Inc., Publishers.
(415) 433-1740; Fax (800) 605-2665.

For sales outside the United States, please contact your local Simon & Schuster International Office.

Jossey-Bass Web address: http://www.josseybass.com

Library of Congress Cataloging-in-Publication Data

Becker, Franklin D.
    Workplace by design: mapping the high-performance workscape / Franklin Becker, Fritz Steele. — 1st ed.
        p. cm. — (The Jossey-Bass management series)
    Includes bibliographical references (p.) and index.
    ISBN 0-7879-0047-8 (acid-free paper)
    1. Office layout. 2. Organizational behavior. 3. Work environment.
I. Steele, Fritz. II. Title. III. Series.
HF5547.2.B39   1994
658.2'3—dc20   94-32960
                                                         CIP

HB Printing   10 9 8 7 6 5 4 3   FIRST EDITION

Contents

Preface

The pace at which organizations are changing is phenomenal. Companies in industries that were once considered staid, such as insurance and banking, as well as those we associate with change and innovation, such as computers and telecommunications, are today speaking common languages. The conversations are about using scarce resources to their fullest potential, about teamwork and cross-functional collaboration, about how to exploit new information technologies for competitive advantage, about changing labor demographics and the implications for attracting and retaining the most qualified staff, about new management strategies and leadership styles, about global strategies and business reengineering.

Change is for most organizations today a matter of survival, and that change is hitting every area of the organization, from executive management to human resources, management of information systems, research and development, marketing and sales, and corporate real estate and facilities management. Competition now comes from all over the world, from people you never heard of, doing things in ways you never thought of.

For most of us, when we hear the word *ecology*, the kinds of images that come to mind are frogs in ponds, wolves bounding through woods, or yellow skies putrid with the pollution from thousands of cars stuck in traffic. Ecology is certainly about organisms' relation to one another and to their surroundings, including the interaction between people and their environment. That environment, however, can be the designed environment we interact with every day at work—our workplace. Just as the wolf or the frog both influence and are affected by their surroundings, so too are we affected by characteristics of our work environment. Its size, shape, layout, quality, furnishings, and equipment shape our work lives, at the same time as our behaviors, attitudes, and values shape the nature of that designed environment, how it is used, and the meanings we attach to it. The ecology of the organization is an often invisible but nonetheless strong force shaping how people work with each other and how well the organization performs, especially when conditions demand flexibility and quick responses to new demands.

Many executives and senior-level managers, overwhelmed with their daily responsibilities, underestimate or misunderstand the role they can and should play in helping create high-performance workplaces. The underlying theme of this book is that organizations that are effective over the long run must create a total workplace in which the physical setting of work, and the processes through which it is planned and managed, get as much executive attention as any other aspect of the business. Good workplaces, from this perspective, are simply good business.

Origins of the Book

There are basically three categories of books concerned with the nature of how the built environment affects individual and organizational performance. One is glossy coffee-table books that focus on office style. These are largely concerned with issues of corporate image, power, and status as communicated through the visual language of design.

A second category is directed toward the architectural and design community, and focuses on techniques for space planning and interior design. These books tend to be written by and for designers and typically concentrate on technical issues related to accommodating information technology, lighting, heating and ventilation, and furniture layout. They discuss the planning and design process to some extent, but from the perspective of the professional designer or facility planner who might lead the design process.

The third category is books that are written for a wider audience, including but not limited to the design community, facility managers, and office workers. These books focus on the individual and organizational consequences of different approaches to office space planning and design, from layout to indoor air quality, and they draw more heavily on systematic research than either of the other two categories. Our own books *(Physical Settings and Organizational Development; Workspace: Creating Environments in Organizations; Making and Managing High Quality Workplaces; The Total Workplace)* fall into this last category.

Over the past twenty years we have studied, written, lectured, and consulted extensively about the importance to organizations of how the physical settings are planned, designed, and managed. Our own books on this subject represent, in fact, a sizable portion of the small literature in this field. While working together over the past seven years, we have realized that a missing segment of the literature is a book that directly targets executives, senior managers, and other opinion leaders.

This book is intended to fill that gap in the literature. It is a natural extension of our own work in this field and addresses an audience that the other books argue should be addressed but so far has not been: executives and other organizational leaders at various levels who set the direction and tone for their organizations; consultants who work with corporate clients to create or improve workplaces; and property developers who increasingly are taking a broader view of what they are creating and how both new (and more often) existing building stock can be transformed, used, and managed over time.

Summary of Key Themes

The main themes of the book can be summarized as follows:

- Organizational leaders need to understand facility issues in business terms and in terms of their impact on the social system of the organization.

- Planning and designing high-performance workplaces are key elements in business planning, and they need executive leadership.

- How the planning and design process is developed and managed is as important as the physical design that results from it.

- The typical workplace constrains organizational effectiveness.

- Well-designed and well-planned workplaces make organizations more competitive.

- As a work setting, an effective organization is best managed as a total integrated system that includes the physical facility, information technology, organizational policies and practices, and management style.

By demonstrating more innovative ways to think about typical organizational dilemmas such as the management of status, control of image, communication, and change, this book should help organizational leaders more effectively manage:

- Their own roles in the planning, design, and management of the workplace; when they should and should not intervene to benefit the organization.

- The organization's scarce resources to their fullest potential.

- The consequences of workplace-related designs and decisions.

- Their responses to the recommendations and activities of internal staff and consultants who propose planning and design approaches to the organization.

Overview of the Contents

The book is organized into two parts. Part One, The Workplace as a Tool for Achieving Goals, introduces the concept of organizational ecology and discusses how it can contribute to organizational effectiveness. Chapter One describes some of the essential characteristics of a high-performance workplace, in particular the importance of thinking of the workplace as a system that depends on the integration of physical settings, work processes, organizational culture, and information technologies to prosper in a tough and turbulent marketplace. Chapter Two identifies and defines the key characteristics of organizational ecology, with particular emphasis on rethinking how we define and measure performance and effectiveness. We suggest criteria for organizational health that broaden the range of performance measures organizations can use to assess whether their workplace is contributing to the organization's overall competitive position.

Chapters Three through Eight then present examples of new ways of working—including team and collaborative environments, nonterritorial offices, telework centers, and home-based telecommuting—that corporations based in the United States, England, Japan, and Europe have implemented to help them use their available resources more effectively. Chapter Nine, Developing an Integrated Workplace Strategy, provides a conceptual framework that ties together these new ways of working into a comprehensive strategic view of workplace strategies, and then it describes the kind of changes organizations are going to have to make if they want to implement an integrated workplace strategy.

Part Two, Putting Space to Work, discusses the planning processes and leadership roles that are needed to transform the principles of organizational ecology into a vital component of overall organizational competitiveness. Chapters Ten and Eleven emphasize the importance of the up-front planning process and of avoiding the tendency to jump to thinking about solutions before the problem is clearly defined. Chapter Twelve examines the concept of workplace quality and argues that it is important not to fall into the trap of thinking that new is always better. Chapter Thirteen summarizes all of the key points made earlier in the book in a series of short and simple recommendations for organizational leaders who want to create high-performance workplaces.

Acknowledgments

The ideas and examples in this book are a result of work we have done over a twenty-year period, involving hundreds of companies and site visits, thousands of formal and informal interviews, and countless discussions with friends, colleagues, and professional acquaintances. There is, of course, no way to thank individually everyone who in ways small and large has made a contribution to our thinking about organizational ecology.

Our ideas have been influenced, in particular, by Frank Duffy, the current president of the Royal Institute of British Architects and a pioneer in considering the organizational implications of office planning and design; by Charles Handy, who has written eloquently about the changing nature of the corporate world; and by Robert Sommer, one of the founders of the field of environmental psychology, whose concern for creating architecture that is humane and dignifies the lives of those touched by it remains a bedrock of our own thinking.

Under the direction of Professor Becker, much of the research cited in this book is based on work done at the Cornell University International Workplace Studies Program (IWSP), which has since 1989 been systematically investigating the ecology of new ways of working in companies in the United States, England, Europe, and Japan. We are indebted to the past and present staff of the IWSP including Bethany Davis, Kristin Quinn, and Andrew Rappaport, as well as to the many corporate and government sponsors of the research program. Our sponsors have been, in a word, terrific. In many cases what started out as a simple contractual relationship has evolved into a long-lasting friendship because of their enthusiasm and support.

A number of people and groups have directly contributed to the shape and feel of this book. They include Laurie Coots, Lenny Nissensen, Alan Drake, John Holey, and Bill Sims, all of whom read very early drafts of the book and gave us invaluable feedback on everything from content and tone to how the book is structured. We are indebted to Christopher Budd, who did the illustrations for the book with good humor and very short notice. And finally, from the day the original book proposal was submitted to the final preparation of the manuscript, Sarah Polster and Barbara Hill, our editors at Jossey-Bass, have given us the rare blend of straight-from-the-shoulder feedback with unwavering support for our original concept. The result is a book that we recognize as our own voice, but is better as a result of listening to theirs.

February 1995

Franklin Becker
Ithaca, New York

Fritz Steele
Brookline, Massachusetts

The Authors

Franklin Becker is professor of human-environment relations and facility planning and management and director of the International Workplace Studies Program in the College of Human Ecology at Cornell University. He earned his B.A. degree (1968) in psychology and his Ph.D. degree (1970) in social and environmental psychology at the University of California, Davis.

Becker's main research activities over the past fifteen years have focused on examining the individual, group, and organizational implications of innovative approaches to planning, designing, and managing the workplace. He has published articles on the ecology of new ways of working, including nonterritorial and team offices, telework centers, home-based telecommuting, and strategies for planning and managing innovative work settings. He has written five books, including *Workspace: Creating Environments in Organizations* (1981) and *The Total Workplace: Facilities Management and the Elastic Organization* (1990).

Becker is a fellow of the American Psychological Association, has received the Distinguished Author award from the International Facility Management Association, and is a principal in @WORK Consulting Group, a consulting firm that works with organizations to help develop and implement innovative workplace strategies.

Fritz Steele is a private consultant on organizational and environmental change and a founding partner of the Portsmouth Consulting Group. He received his B.S. degree (1960) from Yale University and his Ph.D. degree (1965) in organization studies from the Sloan School of Management at the Massachusetts Institute of Technology. He was formerly a member of the faculties of Yale University, Harvard's Graduate School of Education, and most recently the Radcliffe Seminars.

Steele's main professional activities include consultation, executive education, and writing in the areas of organizational development, diagnosis and change of organizational culture, and organizational ecology. He has written numerous articles and books in these areas, including *Physical Settings and Organizational Development* (1973), *The Feel of the Workplace* (1977, with S. Jenks), *The Sense of Place* (1983), and *Making and Managing High-Quality Workplaces* (1986).

Steele is a member of the American Psychological Association and the Organization Development Network. He has also served for a number of years as a member of the board of directors of the Corporate Design Foundation, a Boston-based organization dedicated to increasing the linkage between business practice and effective design of products, corporate communications, and workplaces.

Workplace by Design

PART ONE

THE WORKPLACE AS A TOOL
FOR ACHIEVING GOALS

CHAPTER ONE

Space: The Organization's Second Most Expensive Resource

We hear and read a great deal these days about high-performance teams. We hear much less often about the physical context in which these teams develop and function. Yet just as a Ferrari performs much better on a well-paved road than on a sandy beach, a high-performance team or organization requires a high-performance workplace. But what does that high-performance workplace look and feel like? Think back to your schoolroom when you were in the second or third grade; or if you have young children in first grade or kindergarten, drop by someday and take a close look at their classroom. Chances are, if it is a good school, you will be looking at a high-performance workplace.

What do you see? The room is divided into activity areas, each with its own distinct character. In one corner there is a quiet reading area, with cushions and carpet, and kids absorbed in books, their bodies contorted into every conceivable position. In another corner, there is a sink and counter and a linoleum floor; kids are making clay figures, laughing and chatting.

The teacher's desk, up front but not in the center of the room, is probably empty. The teacher is more likely to be found walking around the room, looking at what the kids have done, giving instructions or praise to individuals and small groups, or listening to one child talk about what she is working on. A teacher's assistant may be working with a small group of children in another room, or helping with math skills in yet another corner, where individual desks are pulled together to form a kind of cloverleaf, with the kids in the group all facing each other. Some children may be found glued to a computer screen, actively exploring the relationship between shapes and sounds, using an interactive computer program.

If you came back later that same day you might find all the desks pushed to the perimeter and the kids all sitting together on the floor in the center of the room, listening to the teacher read a story. The overall impression is one of a pleasant buzz, people working together and alone; sitting, standing, walking, lying down; different activities drawn to different parts of the classroom by special props like cushions, running water, computers, desks. It all seems natural.

What you are looking at, in effect, is a high-performing learning organization. Physical setting, technology, work processes, management style, and organizational philosophy and values are in harmony. Together, they create a dynamic workplace system that supports diversity in work patterns, values cooperation and collaboration, encourages creativity and hard work, and measures a specialized kind of performance. We call it human development.

These kinds of high-performance workplaces exist in schools everywhere. What marks them as such is not that they are all alike, with the same kinds of chairs, tables, or play areas laid out in identical ways, with teachers cloned from a single wizard. It is that the workplace system— people, work processes, technology, organizational culture and practice, and the physical setting—easily and comfortably enhances the performance of a range of people engaged in tremendously diverse activities in pursuit of a clear goal.

These kinds of high-performance workplaces also exist in corporations. This book describes some of the forms they are taking in corporations throughout the United States, as well as in Europe and Asia. In over twenty years' experience consulting with and studying large and small organizations in industries ranging from child care, counseling, health care, and financial services to aircraft engines, computers, and contract furniture, we have seen a dramatic increase in interest in and commitment to creating high-performance workplace systems.

Necessity, as they say, is the mother of invention, and for many organizations over the last decade the necessity has been to reinvent themselves in response to fierce competition. Chrysler and Ford in the auto industry and Steelcase in the contract office furniture industry are examples of companies that reinvented themselves by fundamentally rethinking and redesigning their product development processes. Other companies are doing it by reengineering their creative teams (the advertising agency Chiat/Day), their sales functions (IBM), and their management consulting divisions (the consulting firms Ernst and Young and Andersen Consulting).

These are works in progress—as they should be. Changing an organization, as anyone who has tried knows, is tough work. Our own backgrounds and interests are in organizational behavior, corporate training programs, executive leadership development, the planning, design, and management of the workplace, and the ways in which information technology and organizational culture affect all of these. As a result, we have for many years viewed the organization as a complex, dynamic, living organism whose performance depends on the successful integration and deployment of not just people and technology but also of time and space. All of these are precious organizational resources, and they all need to be carefully and deliberately managed. The executive leadership of a company can decree teamwork and collaboration as the path to quality, as many have done over the past decade. But simply proclaiming teamwork is insufficient. Organizations must be willing to devote the time, money, and energy to create a workplace that has the necessary combination of meeting rooms, team rooms, and interaction areas to transform management philosophy into corporate practice.

As organizational consultants and students of organizations, we have spent most of our professional careers working with organizations to create high-performance workplaces. Our interest in the ecology of the workplace stems in large part from observing how difficult, but important, it is to think of the workplace as a single integrated system, not as a box filled with different parts: incentive systems, information technologies, strategic planning processes, sales training, office layout, financial accounting, purchasing. Gradually, having worked with dozens of companies, we came to realize that what we were doing did not fit existing labels such as organizational behavior, human resources, management of information systems, environmental psychology, or human factors. These were, without a doubt, critical pieces of the puzzle. But the puzzle itself was how to fit them all together in a way that crossed conventional academic and corporate boundaries.

The result, which we reached independently but about the same time, was the creation of what we came to call "organizational ecology." Basically, this means looking at organizations in terms of how work and workers are convened in space and time and how those kinds of decisions both affect and are affected by decisions about the nature of information technology, the design of work processes, human resource policies and practices, and ultimately the organization's philosophy and values.

We know that humans are remarkably adaptive. But the workplace should not, like a 747 airplane on a transatlantic flight, test the limits of human adaptability. We have seen an Alitalia flight turned into an Italian piazza at 35,000 feet. Clumps of passengers—two, three, four, five, six—were laughing and talking everywhere. People strolled up and down the aisles, not on their way to the toilet, but just taking air, flitting from seat to seat in perpetual search of social contact. What a wonderful example of behavior overcoming environmental constraints. It is hard to imagine a setting more designed to limit social discourse than a 747, and yet by force of culture the aluminum tube was transformed into a piazza, full of life, the smell of espresso, the sounds of people having a good time, all with the earth just a speck below.

The problem is not that people cannot overcome their surroundings. We all do, in ways conscious and unconscious, with efforts large and small. From repositioning the desk and bringing in a cushion for the chair to voting with our feet to avoid places that are ugly and uncomfortable, we comment on our surroundings. We cope, but the cost can be high. Overcoming places that reduce our effectiveness and threaten our dignity always takes time and energy.

This book is dedicated to the creation of high-performance workplaces that energize managers and employees alike, to workplaces that use the available resources—people, time, money, technology—to make organizations more competitive so that they not only survive but thrive in difficult and turbulent times. It is about understanding how space, the second most expensive resource an organization has (its people being the first), can be leveraged to help those people work more effectively, and to attract and retain the right people in the first place.

Our underlying theme is that effective, and certainly innovative, high-performance workplaces require executive leadership: well-informed and committed executives and senior-level managers who have a vision of how the workplace can make their organization more competitive. Over the long run, for an organization to use all its resources to their fullest potential requires creating a total workplace in which the physical setting of work, policies about use patterns, and the processes through which it is planned and managed over time get as much executive attention as any other aspect of the business.

The reason is simple: when planned, designed, and managed with imagination, the workplace becomes a fundamental element of the business and its competitiveness. People like Lee Iacocca, the recently retired head of Chrysler, and Jan Carlzon, the president of Scandinavian Airline Systems, both of whom created workplaces to support new work processes, knew this intuitively. Both created stunning new buildings that were designed not merely to house employees nor simply to make a grand corporate gesture. Rather, the buildings were conceived as fundamental organizational tools to promote and support the kinds of teamwork and cross-departmental and cross-discipline interaction both executives knew were critical to their long-term success. One measure of this, for Chrysler, is that the development time for the Neon, the first car to be designed from the ground up in the Chrysler Technology Center, was cut from an industry average of five years to thirty-one months. Significant cost savings were realized on the Neon because of the reduction in development time made possible because of synergies of the cross-functional platform team and the state of the industry Tech Center, the world's only facility to house all car development processes under one roof.

Good facilities will not guarantee success, nor will poorly designed ones guarantee failure. The same can be said for management, employees, and equipment. By themselves, none of these elements of a business is enough to ensure success. They are part of an integrated system, and to function effectively all the parts have to be in harmony. A Porsche without brakes isn't much of a car; a person without a brain isn't much of a human. And not just any brakes or any brain will do. They need to be matched to the other components of the system and suited to the nature of the function they are designed to perform. The same is true of high-performance workplaces.

Given our view that a high-performance workplace is neither like a tent, merely providing shelter from the elements, nor like a necklace, a form of decoration or statement of status, it is not surprising that this book bears little relation to glossy coffee-table editions that focus on office style and the glories of corporate image, power, and status. Nor does it concentrate in depth on more technical issues related to architecture and design, such as human factors and ergonomics, indoor air quality, space planning and furniture layout, accommodating information technology, or providing proper lighting, heating, and ventilation. All of these topics must be addressed in any project, but we have left their detailed discussion to more technical books. Our focus is on the set of organizational and management issues that creates the context for such technical solutions. These issues have to do with organizational direction, the planning and design process, role relationships, the nature of control and influence, organizational culture, empowerment, and policies governing the allocation and use of space. In other words, they concern the nature of leadership.

We believe that providing organizational leaders with real examples of the innovative ways leading-edge organizations have used the planning, design, and management of the workplace to resolve typical organizational dilemmas—dilemmas that range from containing costs and addressing employee concerns about rank and status to improving teamwork, communication, and collaboration—can help them create high-performing workplaces. If, having read this book, organizational leaders understand how the well-designed and well-managed workplace can enhance their organization's competitiveness, we will have succeeded.

CHAPTER TWO

Understanding
Organizational Ecology

Like many large American companies, Chemco (a pseudonym) had over the years become a lumbering behemoth. Fed by the stream of profits generated by many of its products, which were household names, Chemco did not worry about its operating costs. Employees were treated extremely well, and no expense was spared to provide staff with what was considered to be a high-quality working environment. At a time when much of corporate America sat in scaled-down, open-plan work stations (that is, offices formed by using interlocking three- to six-foot-high panels which support work surfaces and storage cabinets), staff at Chemco occupied spacious closed offices. Yet by the beginning of the 1990s Chemco was under enormous pressures to reduce its costs. Competition was up and profits were down. For the first time in its history, people were being laid off.

The old culture was under siege. Senior management wanted costs drastically cut, and they wanted to initiate new ways of working that encouraged teamwork and collaboration while empowering staff to make more decisions and take more responsibility. The staid, hierarchical culture that was Chemco's tradition was to be replaced through reengineering with a more nimble, flatter, and more democratic organization which used fewer resources to greater advantage.

Chemco's story is the story of organizations everywhere. It included what have become familiar forces for change:

- Stronger competition both nationally and internationally.

- Declining productivity, with expenses racing ahead of revenue.

- A workforce that was much more diverse in age, gender, ethnicity, and household composition. In simple terms, a workforce that had more older workers, dual-income households, single parents, women with young children, and people of color.

- A new interest in teamwork and collaboration as products and services became more complex and more expensive to develop at the same time that the need to speed up the development process was increasing.

- A more stringent regulatory environment that made concerns such as traffic congestion and air pollution corporate, not just community, issues.

- An onslaught of new information technologies that seemed to offer limitless possibilities for improving productivity but that also absorbed financial resources at an alarming rate: for the machines and software themselves, for cabling and environmental systems to compensate for increased power and heat loads, for networking systems together, for training people to use the technology, and for maintaining and upgrading the technology continually.

- New management philosophies and practices that encouraged pushing authority and responsibility lower in the organization, decentralizing decision making, and involving more rank-and-file staff.

- And, of course, cost reduction, primarily through reducing headcount but also by consolidating people into fewer buildings, reducing space standards, restricting equipment purchases, and reengineering the business processes themselves to make them more efficient.

Facing this formidable set of pressures, Chemco established a small team charged with exploring ways of reducing costs and encouraging new ways of working; the goal was to promote teamwork by redefining how teams functioned, not only in terms of the business process, but in terms of where they worked and how they worked.

A small, prototype team environment was established. Space was not so much saved as redistributed to support the kind of informal communication and teamwork that Chemco's management viewed as critical to long-term success. Private, enclosed offices about 150 square feet in size were exchanged for small personal harbors 48 square feet in size organized around a common meeting area with tables for impromptu meetings, rolling white boards and tack space, and work tables equipped with powerful computers that could be used by individuals or by a few people working together. Team members were allowed to work at home whenever they felt they could be more productive there, and Chemco gave them a computer and high-speed modem for use at home so they could stay in contact with the office.

While top management had decreed that some form of prototype team environment would be implemented, all members of the team were directly involved in the process for shaping the form the team environment took. The team planned the layout of work areas, including the way storage and messages were handled, and set up rules and policies for how different areas within the team room would be used and how home working would be managed. The result was that the pilot group coalesced faster as a team, communication improved, team members reported less job-related stress, and the team took more responsibility for managing its own progress and disciplining its own members.

Organizational Ecology

Chemco's transformation of the physical workplace to support new business processes is what organizational ecology is about. It includes the ways in which organizational leaders consciously and deliberately make decisions about the form of their buildings: the choice of furnishings; the arrangement of offices and work stations; the layout of circulation; the number and location and character of conference and meeting rooms, stairwells, elevators, cafeterias, and break areas; choices about how and to whom space is allocated; and the nature of the processes used to plan, design, and manage all of these workplace elements over time. In short, organizational ecology is about how an orga-

nization's leaders choose to convene their employees in space and time
in pursuit of a long-term competitive edge.

The three key elements of organizational ecology are:

1. Decisions about the physical settings in which work is
carried out.

2. Decisions about the processes used for planning and designing the workplace system.

3. Decisions about how space, equipment, and furnishings are
allocated and used over time.

All these decisions must be made while taking into consideration these
factors:

• The nature of the work and business processes themselves.

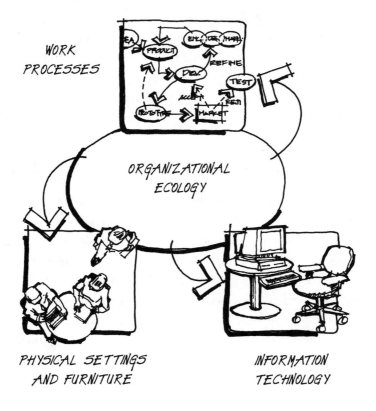

WORK
PROCESSES

ORGANIZATIONAL
ECOLOGY

PHYSICAL SETTINGS
AND FURNITURE

INFORMATION
TECHNOLOGY

- The particular organizational culture and corporate values in which the work is carried out.

- Externalities such as air quality and transportation demand regulations that affect how employees come to work and where they work.

- Real estate supply and demand that affect the cost of space and thus how it is used and where it is located.

- Safety, security, and other quality-of-life issues that affect both where and when people want to work.

- Workforce demographics such as age, gender, household composition, and lifestyle that influence work styles and work locational preferences.

Thus the nature of the physical workplace is only one set of elements to consider in designing the overall ecology of the workplace. Changes in any of these kinds of factors are likely to stimulate changes in the ecology itself. A workforce with an average age of twenty-five, not uncommon in software development firms, is likely to have a different set of pressures than one where the average age may be over forty, not uncommon in the insurance industry. A firm located in southern California faces a different set of external pressures, especially around air quality and transportation demand, than one located in Iowa. The particular form the workplace system takes is shaped by the unique combination of these kinds of factors.

Organizational Ecology and the Total Workplace

In thinking about the nature of the workplace, the characteristic that most distinguishes organizational ecology from the more traditional disciplines of organizational behavior (including human resources, organizational development, human factors, architecture and engineering, and industrial engineering) is concern for the total workplace; this concern draws on all these disciplines but is broader in its scope than any one of them individually.

Organizational ecology must consider organizational behavior issues such as incentive systems, performance appraisal, promotion, formal and informal communication, corporate culture, organizational structure and size; human factors issues such as lighting, noise, ventilation, and air quality; architectural and interior design issues such as how space is designed and allocated and the nature of furniture, materials, and finishes; and industrial engineering issues such as the layout and design of work areas to support work processes.

Organizational ecology seeks to consider these elements of a workplace system as part of an integrated workplace strategy that defines a total workplace in two distinct ways: through the scope of the physical settings considered and through the social processes used to plan and manage—and link—the physical settings over time.

The Total Workplace

As the Chemco case suggests, organizational ecology is concerned with the total workplace. Within this framework, the workplace is not simply one's desk, office, or work station in an office building. It is also the cafeteria, the conference and break rooms, the project room, corridors and water fountains, the fitness center. It is *all the places* in which one works. In today's world, because of the increasing percentage of knowledge workers, that is likely to encompass not just every area within an office building, but cars, hotels, restaurants, airports and airline clubs, the home, satellite office—just about any place one can think, write, talk, or read.

The total workplace is about process as well as product. How the workplace is planned and designed influences the form of the workplace, in terms of its physical design and equipment. But decisions about who is involved and how will have a major influence on employees' understanding of how the system should work once implemented and their commitment to the design concept and intended way of working. Designing a process in which only top management participates will create not just a different physical workplace, but a different set of working relationships than one that involves supervisory staff and all the professional and support staff. How different stakeholders are involved is equally important. Are they merely informed of decisions made by others? Do they provide input, review preliminary plans, give final approval?

The total workplace concept within the organizational ecology framework suggests that organizations need to conceive the workplace as a system of loosely coupled settings that are linked by the physical movement of people and the electronic movement of information in a way that enhances the organization's ability to meet its fundamental business objectives.

Chemco's new team environment, for example, addresses almost all of the pressures noted earlier that organizations are facing. Reducing the size of private work areas made it possible to provide generous shared, common areas without increasing the overall amount of square feet *(cost avoidance)*; team areas reinforced the shift from a focus on individual performance to the performance of the team as a whole *(teamwork)*; an interactive, hands-on planning process for the design of the setting in which all team members participated pushed authority and responsibility for decisions down to those directly affected by them *(empowerment)*; providing drop-in space for noncore support team members within the team area helped break down departmental barriers and spatial isolation *(cross-functional collaboration)*; allowing team members to work at home reduced commuting and enabled those with young children at home to spend more time with them *(workforce demographics; environmental regulations)*.

In the case of an innovative, experimental pilot project like the one at Chemco, the nature of organizational ecology is fairly easy to see. But although perhaps less visible, it operates in every workplace, no matter how grand or ordinary.

The difference between two office buildings on two sides of the Atlantic illustrates in another context just what we mean by organizational ecology.

Philip Johnson's AT&T (now Sony) building on Fifth Avenue in New York City is all surface, all about form and style as art. Its "Chippendale" post-modernist tower symbolizes a return to an earlier era reflected in landmarks such as the Chrysler and Empire State buildings. These self-assured buildings scream corporate power and affluence. We crane our necks up at them and simply marvel.

And what of the insides, where people actually do their work? The rows upon rows of individual open-plan work stations in parade-ground formation standing fast with military discipline contrast starkly with enclosed executive offices. The language of the building's interior layout speaks of hierarchy, individual effort, the need for scheduling, and differences in status and worth. As originally conceived, it perfectly reflected a model of organizational structure and style promoted by Frederick Taylor and his principles of scientific management in the early part of this century, and then polished by major American corporations for the next seventy-five years.

The NMB Bank (now the NMB/Post) building south of Amsterdam, in the Netherlands, is a different sort of landmark. It, too, by its size and sheer novelty, expresses power, self-confidence, and affluence. But its ten towers, none with a right angle, sitting like a modern castle in an urban field, were shaped by the philosophies of Rudolf Steiner, the European educator who advocated the development of emotions as a foundation for intellect. The outside, like AT&T's, turns its back on the formal geometry of the modernist movement. But the form of the building—inside and out—is less driven by the desire to make aesthetic statements than the desire to create a more humane, emotionally enriching setting where life is affirmed and nurtured, not merely lived out.

Water gently flows down open copper channels in the handrails, so that you can dangle your fingers in the water while moving around the building; herbs for the corporate dining table are grown in gardens in the courtyard through which staff can meander; all materials are natural. Work areas are small. They accommodate between fifteen and twenty-five people in a small open room where free-standing systems furniture is arranged in small clumps, often with desks oriented so workers can see and talk with each other. There are no panels separating staff from each other, nor are there huge expanses of work stations in rooms the size of football fields. Conference and meeting rooms are airy and beautiful, even opulent, but executive and management offices are few in number.

Here, too, the layout and furnishings speak volumes about the organization's values, philosophies, and conception of work and workers. The language is one of teams and teamwork, of minimal status and hierarchy, of a concern for the dignity and comfort of the entire staff, of a belief that an enriching environment ultimately benefits the company.

Chemco, the new Sony headquarters, and the NMB Bank all reflect organizational ecology in action. So does every ordinary workplace, whether a branch sales office, the claims division of an insurance company, or the human resources floor in a corporate headquarters.

We take it for granted that the design of our own homes affects how we and our families function, and yet often underestimate the effects our surroundings have on us at work. Why? In part, decisions about the nature of the workplace are viewed by many organizational leaders as *technical* decisions, best left to experts like architects, engineers, and facilities managers; as *financial* decisions, in which cost is the primary concern; or as *political* decisions, definitely within the purview of organizational leaders but made as much on the basis of power and influence as on information about how the decisions are likely to affect organizational performance.

Combined with knowledge about individual and group behavior, these factors are the elements, the kit of parts, that together constitute the raw materials of organizational ecology. How they are organized, which pieces are included or emphasized, and how they are shaped and used in practice define not just organizational ecology but ultimately organizational effectiveness.

Creating high-performance workplaces requires organizational leaders who have the courage to look at financial and political considerations within the context of the organization's longer-term competitiveness. That competitiveness ultimately depends on the most expensive resources the company has, its employees. And those employees' performance, varying from the obvious to the fairly inconspicuous, from communication and commitment to efficiency and comfort, is affected by the nature of their surroundings. Not being able to communicate with a colleague when you need to either delays the project or means pressing on without the necessary input. Executives isolated from their staff and other organizational members lose touch with the pulse of the company without knowing it, and make decisions that would be different if they had regular access to a wider range of information from more diverse sources. From the employees' perspective being excluded from a planning process tends to leave them less committed to working hard at making the plans succeed.

The examples are endless, but the point is simple. It does not take a mammoth dysfunction to grind an otherwise well-oiled machine to a stop. Unattended, a minor oil leak eventually causes the engine to seize up. Fixing the leak before the race starts is infinitely less expensive than replacing the engine after it has failed and the race is lost. To avoid creating organizations that eventually seize up in the face of stiff competition takes leaders who are self-conscious about their own roles in shaping a high-performing workplace, aggressive about involving people throughout the organization, and open-minded about understanding the actual effects of designs and policies, as opposed to their assumed effects.

The Measurement Trap

Managers in today's organizations would be derelict in their duty if they were not deeply concerned about cost containment and reduction. Five years ago IBM sales divisions were measured by the amount of revenue they generated. No one actually knew or cared much about the actual costs of producing the products or delivering the services. But the days when a company like IBM could worry about revenue without respect to costs have passed. IBM now knows precisely how much what it is selling costs, and targets are set not for revenue but for profitability. That makes sense. Trying to justify every cost in relation to revenue is, however, not always easy or necessarily the wisest thing to do. Demanding hard evidence for guaranteed productivity gains before doing anything new can stop innovation in its tracks.

Trying to understand what some activity or event or design feature can contribute to organizational effectiveness is perfectly legitimate. But defining the bottom line primarily in financial terms, and then using it as the basis for justifying innovation, can be counterproductive.

Faced with the bottom-line challenge, people react in fascinating ways. Some seek divine deliverance: "Please, God, deliver to me convincing evidence that new furniture will save the company $1.3 million through increased productivity so I can demonstrate a two-year payback." If the case can be made for a direct cost savings, so much the better. But if it cannot, it makes more sense to reframe the debate.

REFRAMING THE DEBATE

There is a wonderful apocryphal story about the scientists of the University of Chicago Fermi Lab, designed to study nuclear fusion. To convince Congress to support the enormously expensive project, at the time one of the largest requests ever made for government support of a scientific enterprise, the scientists redrew the boundaries of the debate. While testifying before a congressional committee, the lead scientist was asked the question traditionally used as the acid test: how would this project contribute to national security? The expected response would have been an invented, or at least exaggerated, statement of some untestable national security benefits. Instead his response was something like this: "Sir, I am not sure there are any national security implications. However, I would say this: It is just this kind of project that makes this country worth defending." He shifted the boundaries and redefined the debate, from national security to national pride. He also won congressional support for the project.

It takes a lot of confidence to challenge "the way we do things here," but we have seen it work, and work well. It requires evidence, but this evidence can take many different forms. If the real goal is innovation, and in many organizations today survival dictates that it must be, then the definition of the bottom line needs to be drawn more broadly. In the context of innovation, focusing exclusively on hard evidence like return on investment or keeping to a tight project schedule even when it precludes creative experiments makes a virtue out of tilting at windmills. What's needed is a collaborative redefining of the relevant measures, perhaps within a larger set of corporate values than the ones being articulated by those invoking the (cost and schedule) bottom line. If nothing else, the process itself provides the invaluable service of forcing senior management to understand the choices they are actually making, and it gives them the opportunity to make a genuinely informed decision about the allocation of resources.

CONSENSUS PERFORMANCE MEASURES

An excellent book by Robert Brinkerhoff and Dennis Dressler (1990) called *Productivity Measurement: A Guide for Managers and Evaluators* lists four useful criteria to consider in developing any type of productivity measurement. The four criteria are:

1. *Quality*. Any measures used must define and reflect quality of product or services as well as quantity. Reducing unit manufacturing costs does not make sense if it results in high levels of product defects, increased warranty costs, and loss of consumer confidence. In the case

of Chemco, the ultimate test of the new workplace strategy will be the extent to which the new business system being developed works for those using it (internal customers). Was the product developed faster than similar products in the past? Does it speed response time to inquiries, have fewer glitches in the program compared to past efforts, make tracking and analysis of data easier? No single case can answer the question definitely, but if the same approach is used by different teams, for different products and services, and it consistently shows improvements on these quality indices, it becomes safe to conclude that the differences are not just a function of a particular manager, or a few talented team members, or the nature of the particular task.

2. *Mission and Goals.* Measures must assess behaviors, events, activities, or outcomes that are perceived to help the organization achieve its fundamental business objectives; they must be integral to the company's mission and strategic goals. For a service-oriented company that believes that customer contact generates good ideas as well as higher sales, a measure of "face time" with customers makes a lot of sense; for others it may not. In Chemco's case this would mean measuring, with surveys and interviews and focus groups, whether communication and collaboration were improved, whether there were more and faster communication turnarounds among core team members and between them and those supporting the core team with their specialized expertise.

3. *Rewards and Incentives.* Measures must be integrated with and reflect performance incentives, reward systems, and practices. If "willingness to challenge others' ideas" typically results in someone being labeled "difficult" or "not a team player" or "insubordinate," then this is not a good measure to use. At Chemco team members were encouraged to solve their own problems; in effect, to bypass their immediate supervisor and take on responsibility for their own group's effectiveness. The behaviors made easier by the new spatial organization—the open, shared team room made each team member's performance much more visible than it had been previously, when everyone occupied individual closed offices—were in this case valued and rewarded.

4. *Employee Involvement.* Employees and other direct stakeholders must be involved in proposing and choosing productivity measures. Without this involvement there will be no buy in, and it is likely that the

data collected will be challenged as irrelevant or biased. At Chemco commitment to more informal communication and collaboration, to helping others solve problems, and to being accessible was clearly understood as desirable behavior by supervisors, managers, and team members, who talked about those behaviors as part of the planning process for the new team environment.

Meeting these criteria requires, by definition, that the organization have a clear mission statement and philosophy about how the mission is best achieved and that the company's formal values and stated philosophy are more than wall decorations. In addition to the criteria set forth by Brinkerhoff and Dressler for measuring performance, we have found it useful to use a model called the Criteria of Organizational Health.

CRITERIA OF ORGANIZATIONAL HEALTH

The model has been borrowed loosely from general systems theory, and it is based on thinking of the organization as an organism that needs multiple factors to be in balance in order to survive and succeed. The model assumes that using one single indicator of the health of an organization is like asking someone whether he prefers his heart or his lungs. It's a stupid question. Without both organs functioning well, the person will soon die.

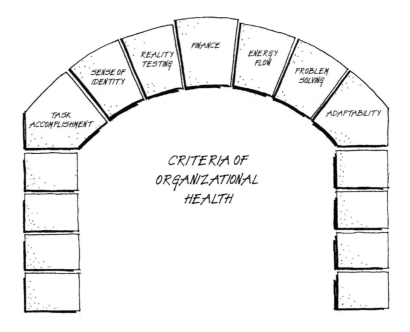

This model is immediately useful as a way of challenging the widespread practice of measuring an organization's health by only one indicator—its economic bottom line. Economic success is obviously an important prerequisite for long-term survival (without it the system runs out of resources), but it is not sufficient; an organization can blow apart while producing strong financial results.

We use the organizational health model to help leaders assess the effects that they are likely to create with spatial decisions, as well as to set specific change goals based on critical problem dimensions.

The following is a brief description of five key criteria of organizational health and some examples of how facilities can influence them.

1. *Sense of Identity*. The members have a clear sense of the organization's mission, values, style, and culture. People outside the system see a clear image of what it does and what it stands for. In terms of membership, it is clear who is in and who is not.

Many kinds of facilities elements can affect this dimension: decorative styles, the location of offices, allocation of space, treatment of boundaries between the system and the outside world, signs, artworks, and so on. The work setting is a powerful medium for expressing identity.

2. *Reality Testing*. Members of the system are able to get timely and accurate information about what is happening, both inside the system and in the surrounding environment. The often-heard call to "manage by walking around" is basically about reality testing: getting off the executive floor and out of the private office to mix with the troops and find out what they are doing and thinking. Healthy systems have formal and informal processes in place for seeking patterns, interpreting them, and sharing them with others. Information gets to the right people at the right time so that effective action can be taken when issues arise.

This criterion is particularly influenced by those workplace features that promote or block communication throughout the organization: adjacencies (relative locations of individuals and groups), communication technologies, patterns of meeting facilities, common facilities that serve as magnets to draw people together on an unplanned basis. The workplace can be a big help in reality testing, but it can also create blocks that impede this process by reducing the probability of regular information sharing, especially between levels or different functional groups. For example, isolated executive floors and dining rooms undermine reality testing, while shared eating facilities and equal access to fitness facilities promote it.

3. *Task Accomplishment.* The system fulfills its mission if it satisfies the expectations of both insiders and outsiders. It therefore receives sufficient new inputs (money, people, information) so as not to run down over time. It does this with an efficient use of resources.

Obviously many facilities factors can have an impact (for better or worse) on the organization's basic tasks: size and quality of individual workplaces, ergonomics, meeting spaces and other areas for joint activities, information and communication technologies, relative locations of different parts and the resulting energy required to have contact, and so on. Task accomplishment may also be affected by the setting's effects on other criteria such as reality testing.

4. *Problem Solving and Adaptability.* As conditions change internally or externally, the system's members are able to make short- or long-term changes that solve problems or seize opportunities created by the changes.

This area is heavily influenced by the degree of flexibility built into work settings, as well as by facility management policies. Shifting from office sizes allocated on the basis of rank to universal same-size offices makes it easy to move people rather than walls or panels. It is also faster, cheaper, and less disruptive. Adaptability is also encouraged by work settings that have a rich variety of different types of activity spaces that people can choose from based on what they are doing at any particular time, instead of many duplicates of the same standard work station that often is poorly designed for either concentrative or interactive work. Settings that foster communication also help members spot problems early on while action is still possible.

5. *Energy Flow.* Members manage the relations among the parts of the system (individuals, groups, levels, and so forth) so that the energy generated by collaboration, conflict, teamwork, tension, and so forth gets used productively rather than draining energy from tasks or splintering the system permanently. This dimension is influenced by relative locations of parts, boundaries between groups, spaces that tend to promote cooperation or competition, and facility policies that influence how people can use their facilities.

These are obviously not five totally independent dimensions. Being out of balance on one can cause problems on other criteria as well (for example, poor reality testing making it difficult to spot and solve problems, or poor energy flow eroding a common sense of identity).

As the following table suggests, using the Criteria of Organizational Health is likely to generate new interpretations about the meaning of how space is allocated and used. The kind of participatory planning process that Chemco used to design its new team space shifts from becoming a waste of valuable employee time to a form of organizational development that strengthens the employees' commitment to the new way of working. A smaller personal office is transformed from a sign of status demotion to a sign of commitment to collaboration and teamwork. The team environment is more likely to be associated with a strong, innovative organization on the cutting edge of new ways of working than one that is solid and conservative.

We don't intend to overplay the metaphor of the organization as a living organism. But new criteria change the context in which actions are interpreted, and over time they can change the culture itself. The main point is that using multiple criteria of organizational health can provide a language for systematically describing and diagnosing problems, setting change goals, and making choices among different workplace strategies or designs. The best approach depends on key issues or demands on the organization, not on generic rights and wrongs.

It also depends on how the system is designed as a whole. Open work stations may make sense if there are also totally private areas for highly concentrative tasks. Informal dress codes in "backstage" areas do not have to undermine a traditional corporate business image if guests are always met in formal conference rooms by employees who have changed for these meetings into standard business attire. Executives can be located together if they structure times to meet regularly with their staff in the staff areas. Thinking of the organization in this way creates many more choices and opens opportunities to create new work patterns as much by changing use patterns as by physically redesigning the workplace.

Old vs. New Assumptions Using the Criteria of Organizational Health.

OLD ASSUMPTIONS	NEW ASSUMPTIONS
One person, one place "owned" by them exclusively.	One person, a number of different places used jointly.
Work happens at the desk, the terminal, or in meetings.	Work happens all day long wherever the person happens to be, in many different spots.
Facilities are best used as rewards or perks for one's level in the system.	Settings are tools to get things done, and as such are too expensive to use as status symbols.
Workplaces should project a certain image to visitors.	Workplaces that are well designed for their users will inherently project the right image.
Personal choice by users about facilities is too slow, complicated, and potentially chaotic.	Appropriate choices by users result in better settings and stronger commitment to using them well.
Saving on space costs is always a gain for the organization because it improves the bottom line.	Space costs should be controlled without compromising the best achievement of overall objectives, which is the organization's reason for existence.

We are not suggesting that every organization should adhere to all of these new assumptions, only that they are directions that tend to move away from the more static views of workplaces and how they can be used. We think that this approach is compatible with a more conscious awareness of workplace impact and the leader's role in keeping it effective over time. It also reflects the basic principles of organizational ecology, as defined earlier; namely, to consider process as well as product, and to see high-performing workplaces as not a single place but as an integrated workplace system that simultaneously considers how decisions about the nature of physical settings, information technologies, work and business processes, and corporate values and philosophies can be shaped in light of workforce demographics and external business conditions to enhance the long-term competitive position of an organization.

Using these criteria as suggestive guides also moves us beyond the simplistic comparison of choices based solely on costs (initial and operating). They help us to include the most important missing part of the equation: the impact on organizational effectiveness that the expenditures will achieve over time. This is, after all, the point of bothering to have the workplace.

CHAPTER THREE

Rethinking Status, Identity, and Space

We all know about status in the office, but Union Carbide's corporate headquarters in midtown Manhattan in the 1970s, like a lot of other corporate headquarters buildings at that time, pushed the connection between status and space to its limits. Every aspect of the office environment was part of a widely understood and sophisticated status language. More space, wooden furniture, better views—all were associated with higher rank. How close you were located to senior management was also a matter of rank, and so was the floor you worked on. These are all fairly conventional ways to communicate status distinctions, but Union Carbide went further. The material your coffeepot or ashtray was made of also connoted status; so did having or not having carpet or wallpaper, and if you did, what color and grade it was.

A promotion in this kind of environment was no simple affair. A move up for one person in a group could trigger an avalanche of moves because of the need to reconfigure and reoutfit the new office so that it perfectly matched the new rank. The system threatened to topple of its own complexity. Trying to dress the office in this way made any kind of reorganization a nightmare. Employees became obsessed in some cases with making sure that their office matched their status in the tiniest detail. In this kind of status-laden world one frequently heard stories of managers complaining because their office was one foot too small. From another organization we have a photograph of an "office" fourteen feet long and six inches wide! The unused space was the result of the company's efforts to ensure that employees of equal status had offices of identical size on either side.

Then, in the early 1980s, Union Carbide built a new headquarters building in Danbury, Connecticut, and made some fairly radical changes. Every office was exactly the same size, for first-level professional or president of a division. The furniture in the offices was not identical, because Carbide wanted all employees to be able to select from a number of furniture packages those that most suited their own work style and sense of identity. All the furniture packages (there were fifteen of them, each in two color combinations) were, however, of comparable cost.

The results were as unusual as the remedy. A study done by Cindy Froggatt (1985) at Cornell University as part of her master's thesis found a higher level of employee satisfaction with the new office environment than had been found in any other published study at the time. The disruption and cost of reconfiguring the environment every time someone was promoted were drastically reduced. Now people, rather than walls (and coffeepots and ashtrays and carpets), were moved.

Union Carbide's transformation of its corporate culture through a transformation of its corporate facilities illustrates a number of organizational ecology principles:

- Decisions about the amount and quality of space and furnishings and materials are a powerful way to express deeply held organizational values—every minute of every day.

- Decisions about the amount and quality of space and furnishings can become an organizational straitjacket, limiting the ways in which the organization functions because it is so expensive or time-consuming or disruptive to make changes.

- Imaginative ways of allocating space and furnishings can support both individual identity needs and organizational cost concerns, two areas that are often thought of as inevitably being in conflict.

As a nonverbal communication system, the way in which the office environment is planned, designed, and managed communicates in

what anthropologist Edward T. Hall (1959) years ago called the
"silent language," a wide range of messages including but not limited
to status, such as:

- The identity of users and of the group or system as a whole.

- The history of the organization (founding myths, key people in its
  history, changes in the nature of the mission, critical events that
  somehow got memorialized).

- Leaders' values about relationships, work processes, important
  goals, and the like; expectations about what should and should not
  happen in the place; and messages about who should and should
  not use it.

Redefining Corporate Image

It is rumored that the reason John Hancock Insurance built its glass
office tower in Back Bay Boston was to provide a (slightly taller and
newer) counterpoint to the Prudential Insurance Company's earlier
office tower. There were obviously many considerations that went into
Hancock's decision, and yet it also had the inevitable flavor of "ours is
bigger than yours," especially since they went to considerable trouble to
build, over many planning objections, such a large structure on unstable
soil in a historic area.

All organizations send messages about their values, aspirations, and
expectations with design choices they make about everything from the
site to the building's exterior size and form and materials, to the details
of how its interior spaces are furnished, arranged, and used. Historically,
many designs have been driven as much by a concern for whether the
building's image is "correct" as by any other factor except sheer numbers of people to be accommodated.

Obviously, a new headquarters should support the basic work being
done there. It should also support the organization's identity. The key
question is the nature of the identity you want to project. Decisions
about the form, location, and nature of the headquarters will communicate to insiders and to the external world how the organization views its

social system: what it is trying to do, managerial values and style, desired stance toward the surrounding community, orientation toward stability and change, and so on. Clarity of statements (images) in these areas can help members identify with and strengthen their commitment to the system, and it can help outsiders know how to relate to the organization. Clarity of identity can also be a help in attracting and keeping people who are essential to the success of the system.

The necessity to make spatial choices also provides a fallout benefit in terms of the discipline that comes from examining one's vision of the organization's mission and style. It is all too easy to put off such self-examination in keeping up with day-to-day operations, but a new headquarters project forces the question. It is very hard to proceed without choosing or confirming an identity as the basis for determining the building form and space planning decisions.

There is an inherent tension in this area between, on the one hand, choosing an image to project and then making a headquarters that will project this image, and, on the other, choosing desired ways of working as an organization, making a good workplace to support that, and letting the result be the image statement, reflecting how the system really works.

We strongly support the latter approach—making workplaces that reflect your goals and work style, thereby letting the image speak for itself. Doing it the other way around requires too much "staging" of scenes for the benefit of observers. This places too much pressure on workers to follow scripts so they look right in terms of the desired image, which in many instances is different from getting on with doing a good job.

If the goal is to have the corporate image reflect the values that guide how the organization really functions (or would like to), then the thrust of the questions asked when starting a building project should be on what you want to *be* as an organization, not on what you want to *look like*. We would suggest that you not even ask the second question, but rather collect members' views on what they think the system is or should be in areas such as core values, work style, management style, and orientation toward employees and the community.

In other words, the focus should be driven by what you want to do, how you want to do it, and what you want work life to be like for everyone. With this approach it is also relatively easy for the organization's different parts to express their own particular styles (by being clear about what they want to do and how) without having to express one monolithic corporate image (unless that *is* how the organization works, with no variations among the parts).

Letting your choices speak for themselves follows the famous dictum of therapist Carl Rogers: "The facts are friendly." In the long run it wastes less energy and generates fewer unnecessary problems if you can be comfortable letting who you are (a person or an organization) show directly without having to stage-manage the impression you are giving to others. If the appearance you are trying to promote doesn't match the reality of how people need and want to work, what probably needs to change is how you *feel* about the reality. If you become more comfortable with the way your organization does things, then there is less need to look like something else.

If letting the image evolve from the way the organization actually works (or would like to) makes so much sense, why are there so many examples of corporate work settings that seem, like the John Hancock building, to represent the opposite approach? Why are elaborate monuments and sculptures created that have either little relation to the work to be done there, or more often a negative feel, stifling many of the activities that would support the organization's mission?

Part of the reason seems to be fear of one's own customers and clients: in particular, the fear that a more diverse corporate image would be interpreted by clients and customers as evidence that the organization is out of control, disorganized, unsure of and possibly at war with itself. Oddly, we cannot think of any corporations that actually test these kinds of assumptions, nor have we heard anyone make such judgments about another organization.

On the contrary, we do know that some corporations have built their corporate images around being different, precisely because their customers and clients appreciate visiting offices that differ from their own fairly uniform, predictable spaces. Architecture and advertising offices often do this. But even in these kinds of offices the focus is often on exterior image—lobbies, cafeterias, executive conference rooms, and so on.

The reality of how the organization works day in and day out is much more evident in what happens not in the high-profile, front-stage areas of lobby, boardroom, and cafeteria but in what life is like in the back-stage areas where people work, where products are created, services delivered, and administration applied. For us, it is these backstage areas that truly reflect an organization's culture, and ultimately its effectiveness as an organization. Why not build the corporate image around these activities and areas?

There are companies, like DEGW, an innovative firm of architects and space planners based in London, that have done precisely this. Clients are not confined to a few stage-managed public areas, whether conference rooms or partners' offices (which do not exist); instead, they are often taken on a tour of the whole firm and meet in the same areas where staff are working and meeting.

What is on display is not so much a design aesthetic—though this is present and was consciously constructed—as it is a way of working expressed through design: fluid, open, dynamic, energetic. The sounds and sights of people talking and meeting, bent over their drawing boards, peering into computer screens, chatting while getting a cup of coffee—all the comings and goings of the office itself are showcased by simple furniture, by an open-plan design, by meeting tables located in highly visible circulation areas. The company is in a renovated warehouse space overlooking the Regent's Canal at the edge of the King's Cross railway station. The location itself, still semiderelict but with enormous potential to become a fashionable new center of activity in the future, is an expression of a risk-taking culture. The whole building showcases the corporate culture; the building *is* the corporate image.

In a much larger office in a completely different business, Digital Equipment Corporation's head offices in Espoo, Finland, play a similar role to DEGW's.* The building itself is unremarkable. Its plain rectangular form looks like any other modern speculative office building, virtually indistinguishable from those around it.

What is remarkable is the interior of what DEC Finland calls its "office of the future." Here, the corporate image is full-flavored, undiluted, and deliberate. But it has little to do with architectural fashion,

---

This office no longer exists, not because it was not valued, but because the new ways of working it reflected reduced the amount of space sufficiently to enable DEC to vacate the annex building it had been leasing.

interior design panache, or novelty for form's sake. Rather, it proclaims a commitment to providing employees with whatever tools they need to get their job done, and to encouraging novelty in work patterns—and the furniture that will support it—that is likely to increase employee effectiveness and productivity.

From swing sets to picnic furniture and easy chairs that tilt back into a reclining position, DEC's offices are the centerpiece of their image. They are intended to dazzle clients and visitors not by displaying power, wealth, and good taste, but by underscoring the commitment to innovation, to using the latest technology, to trusting staff, and to being willing to take risks, all in the service of becoming more productive and serving customers better.

Companies like DEGW and DEC are as concerned with corporate image as any others. The difference is, they are building the corporate image around work patterns that relate to how the organization serves its customers, rather than the more typical testimonial to past achievements or future aspirations. This approach requires confidence that the organization itself is noteworthy, and that customers and clients, and even staff themselves, can be impressed by and attracted to an image that is more than skin deep, that penetrates beyond the facade, the atrium, and the executive conference room to the places that define what the organization is really about. In a sense it suggests daring to believe that someone could take you seriously, because of what you say and do, even if you aren't wearing a three-piece suit.

Removing the Status Straitjacket

Perhaps the most constraining symbolic use of workspace comes not from concern about external messages, but from that ubiquitous medium of internal communication, the language of status symbol. The language is made up of all the rules about provision of space, location, and accoutrements based on a person's standing in the organizational hierarchy. Although using space as a status language is an almost universal practice, there are large unexamined costs in terms of organizational effectiveness and flexibility.

A highly technical company recently formed a multifunction, multilevel project team to plan and implement a major overhaul of its information-processing systems. Since the team members were located in two separate buildings and on different floors of the main building, the project leader considered creating a project team area with all team members located together. He was discouraged from doing this by his boss, on the grounds that there was no way to find an area that would provide all the members the types of workspaces they were entitled to by the company's space standards.

The team leader has tabled the idea and accepted the consequence that it is going to take the project longer to get moving and retard the development of an integrated project team. As he put it, "Practically the only time members see each other, especially from different disciplines, is when we have a scheduled meeting, which is not that often. It's not surprising that they're already starting to burrow into their subparts and leave the integration to fate."

The bind that this manager finds himself in is typical of an extremely widespread pattern in U.S. companies. Leaders' assumptions about the necessity of using personal space, location, and furnishings as rewards and indicators of organizational status place them in a kind of straitjacket with two kinds of constraints: how a total workplace can be designed, and how it can be used. Most of the inertia seems to be social rather than physical: policies and norms about who is allowed to work in which kinds of space and locations. Even people who recognize the clear need for a change often put it off because they don't want to get caught up in the political infighting required to make it happen.

The design constraint is obvious. Once you have satisfied all the requirements for varying sizes of personal workplaces as dictated by the space standards, there is usually a real squeeze placed on providing other kinds of spaces, such as conference rooms, informal conversation areas, and the like. Because of budget constraints these tend to be seen as luxuries to be tacked on after everyone has been given a place. This is not a very good design process, to say the least, but it becomes even less functional when the organization's work calls for people to spend less time in their individual spots and more time working with others.

The constraint on use patterns occurs when managers need to change groupings quickly and redeploy the existing workspaces and activity areas, as in the above example. As the Union Carbide example at the beginning of this chapter suggests, it becomes very difficult to regroup people because it is very likely to violate the rules of entitlement imposed by the space standards. One of two costs is then likely to be incurred: either the facilities cost of restructuring walls, lighting, wiring and furnishings to make the new pattern fit the status language; or the "inertia cost" to performance (to the speed of team development in our example) of not moving people into the new configuration. This latter cost is potentially more damaging to the organization because it is less obvious than the restructuring costs and because it has a cumulative negative effect, accruing over the full time that people are in ineffective arrangements.

Some organizations are already moving away from the strictures of space as status. One approach has been to create one basic size of workplace for everyone, what Aetna Life and Casualty calls "universal plan" offices. These one-size-fits-all work stations are tailored to meet different work styles and job functions by fitting out the standard footprint with different furniture components arranged in different ways. When departments are reorganized the only things that move are people and some furniture components. The time, expense, and disruption of moving walls or panels are eliminated.

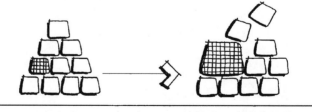

SPACE BY RANK: EFFECT OF PROMOTION

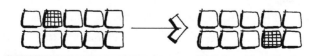

UNIVERSAL PLAN: ONE SIZE FITS ALL

Another approach is to have varied workplaces but allocate them on some basis not tied to rank or status. For example, the members of a small bio-tech firm put all of its workspaces on slips of paper and drew them out of a hat. This got rid of the status tie-ups, and has had the side benefit of helping people to get acquainted with others in different disciplines who had tended to keep to their separate group areas in their previous, more traditional functional group arrangement. To promote this mixing even further, they plan to reshuffle all their spots periodically.

In a variation of this, Arnold and Porter, a prestigious Washington, D.C., law firm, assigned every professional member of the firm a number, based on position and length of service with the company. The person with the highest number could select any office, anywhere in the building. All of the offices were the same size, but some were of different shapes. The person with the next highest number selected any office she wanted from those that were left, and so on down the line. Some people chose offices based on the view, some on the shape of the office, some on whom they would sit next to.

In another of our client companies a number of offices were being shifted around to accommodate several new employees. Some of the offices had windows and very good views; others were on the interior core, with one glass wall looking toward the windowed offices (so that they still got natural light and had a somewhat distant view of outside). The human resources director proposed that she and several others *not* move into the windowed offices they were "entitled" to, since that would mean moving even more people to bump them to a workspace of the appropriate status level. Since the proposed changes were intended to last only about eight months or so, when they intended to do a more thorough redesign, the HR director reasoned that it was wasteful and foolish to play the bumping game.

And yet windows have traditionally been treated as a commodity to be doled out as a reward for status in the system, rather than as a tool for providing for fundamental human needs. Having a workplace with a window is typically treated automatically as a valuable perk to be awarded on the basis of job rank or other status considerations. You can be branded a heretic if you even ask questions about the usefulness of this practice.

From our point of view, it is quite important nonetheless to ask questions about the window game. Adherence to the conventional allocation formula tends to incur two kinds of costs for the organization. One is the constraint on layout, locations of people, and groupings that results from always having to put higher-ranking people around the perimeter of an office area. In terms of group and intergroup interaction, sizing of group spaces, relationships of executives to one another, and so on, this peripheral distribution tends to encourage disconnectedness. It also makes it hard to create appropriate clusters that cut across formal work group lines because there usually aren't enough nearby windowed offices to accommodate the "rights" of the senior members. Quick temporary relocations of people are also difficult (and therefore less likely to be done, even when badly needed) when you have to satisfy the window-allocation rule.

The second kind of cost is somewhat elusive but no less important in terms of this chapter's focus: a degrading of the spirit or climate of the organization. Many members who are excluded see the window game as a visible, constant reminder of an organizational policy that they feel is both arbitrary and unfair. They see people who already have richer job experiences and more freedom to work in alternative places (absence from one's office tends to be correlated with rank) also being handed exclusive rights to natural light and outside views. A company can implement all sorts of programs on employee involvement or empowerment, but rigid adherence to the windows game is a simple daily contradiction of the leaders' good intentions.

This aspect of the windows issue has struck us as being somewhat analogous to the shoreline problem in ocean-bordering states. The status-driven model for allocating windows is like a state allowing the oldest and richest families to own all of the coastline and control access to it, with the rest of the public excluded except by invitation. Extending sunlight as a community commodity rather than a status indicator is to treat as much as possible of the window wall as "public shoreline."

One professional firm we know of moved into an old mill building along the banks of the Charles River near Boston, with views on the river side of the building that were quite beautiful and peaceful. The managing partners decided that it would be a mistake to close these views off from all except a few fortunate individuals (probably themselves) who would typically get offices with windows looking out to the river. Instead, they put a variety of shared common spaces along the window walls: cafeteria, meeting rooms, presentation spaces, informal conversation areas, coffee areas, and walkways. The result is that everyone in the firm has a number of access points for pleasant views while working, chatting, eating, or simply taking a break and hanging about while recharging their batteries. This design also turns out to be highly noticeable, making a strong statement to visitors and occupants that helps to define the climate of the firm.

It seems clear that the decision to make light and views a common resource will tend to enhance overall morale in this firm. It also communicates a kind of thoughtfulness to visitors, who often comment on the departure from the typical way of handling windows and locational decisions. The other payoff from breaking out of the window game is that leaders gain flexibility in both long- and short-term arrangements by not having preset rules about who should be located by windows or in the interior.

The key point is that layouts, workplace design, and locations of individuals and groups are important influences on organizational performance. As such, they should not be overdetermined by the pecking order, which only occasionally will match the configuration needed to get the job done. All locations and facilities should be thought of as a dynamic system, changing as needs change, rather than a relatively fixed allocation of goodies based on rank.

What's the Real Message?

Design choices are either congruent or incongruent with the formal pronouncements of organizations, supporting or contradicting them. In this sense they are a kind of paralanguage. As sociologist Irving Goffman (1959) and many others have pointed out, we tend to pay a great deal of attention to nonsemantic aspects of behavior (*how* did she say "I love you?") and to their nonverbal aspects (was he looking you in the eye, holding you close?) because we believe they are truer indicators of underlying attitudes than the content by itself. The content is under more conscious control, and therefore more likely to be stage managed. The best of all worlds is when the semantic and nonsemantic aspects of speech reinforce each other. Then we really believe the message.

The same is true of our physical surroundings. Even though corporate facilities are very consciously designed at one level, at other symbolic levels they may be much less so. No organization consciously and explicitly wants to tell its employees that it doesn't care a whit about their views on how to be productive. Yet many do this inadvertently by ignoring staff complaints about uncomfortable chairs, poor lighting, stuffy air, and poorly designed work surfaces. The damage is not just in the energy lost in trying to surmount these environmental obstacles, but in the more subtle and longer-lasting impressions such dysfunctional environments generate about the organizational leaders' real attitudes toward high performance, as opposed to concerns for cost or image.

We encountered a particularly poignant example of this kind of conflict recently when interviewing employees in a research group. One of them spoke with great emotion about how bad it felt to be hamstrung in her work by bureaucratic indifference and game playing. She had needed a particular piece of equipment to run a series of tests, and she needed it in a hurry. There was just such a machine sitting two doors away from her in a vacant workspace, but she was ordered not to use it because it would eventually go to another group; and more to the point, she was not authorized to use it because of her level in the hierarchy. She spoke with tears in her eyes about the frustration of wanting to do a good job and being arbitrarily blocked from doing it.

Places like Xerox PARC in Palo Alto, California, and Apple Computer's new research and development center in the heart of the Silicon Valley south of San Francisco, use the same kind of silent language, but to advantage. Here, the rhetoric of creativity, freedom, and nonconformity is perfectly reflected in break areas with comfortable sofas arranged in whatever way they were left by the last group to use them, walls painted with murals by adventurous programmers, and a variety of banners, posters, and knickknacks. An R&D center built with expensive and delicate finishes and laid out in rigid ways would be like a lover whispering "I love you" in a bored voice while doing a crossword puzzle. In high-performance workplaces the environment not only functionally enables desired behaviors to occur, it reinforces the values guiding these behaviors through the silent language of environmental cues.

Employees constantly read the environment for cues about management's real intentions. Those with the opportunity to influence the messages sent by decisions concerning the office environment—and these decisions can be about how space is laid out and used as well as what it looks like or what color it is—need to be very thoughtful about design choices and the processes used to make them. The kinds of resources allocated to users, and the policies established about how they can be used or changed, implicitly lay out a vision or an agenda for changing how the system should work day-to-day. They all are read by employees for messages about intention, values, directions, concerns, and the like, and compared with more explicit written statements such as those found in annual reports and executive memos. When there are discrepancies, the designs and policies are believed before the rhetoric as more genuine indicators of what leaders will really choose to do when the chips are down.

Some examples of the kind of environmental messages that send clear signals about underlying organizational values, intentions, and agendas include:

• If the organization's leaders say they are committed to teamwork and cross-functional collaboration, do they also provide areas that make it easy for group members to meet informally, both within their own teams and across team boundaries? If good places are not provided for such new kinds of work, people hear the rhetoric as nothing more than the "flavor of the month," to be done along with everything else they're already doing. They don't believe they will actually be expected to drop some of the individualistic tasks which have gotten in the way of teamwork.

A　　　　　　　　B

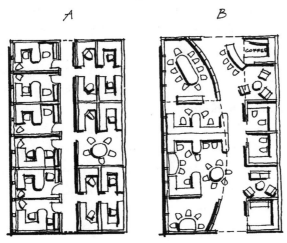

IS TEAMWORK THE MESSAGE?
WHICH OPTION REALLY PROMOTES TEAMWORK?

- If the leaders view their system as a learning organization, do they provide settings and materials for learning and development activities and allow people the time to actually engage in them? Many leaders today talk about how critical it is to survival to be a "learning organization," but few of them engage in the search and provide the resources to actually create such an entity. With respect to individual learning, seminar and lab spaces are often the first to get co-opted as office space when new bodies are added to a growing organization. The message to the troops is again quite clear: learning and reflection are all right as long as we don't have any better uses for our time and spaces.

- If the leaders claim to believe that serendipitous communication and interaction—the water cooler phenomenon—spark new ideas, do they provide areas that promote and facilitate chance encounters? If a layout is done with magnet centers that draw people together, and if the spaces are shaped and sized so that it is easy for people to talk to each other without being uncomfortable or blocking others' movements, then there is a strong message that this sort of community-building contact is indeed valued. Conversely, if no centers are created or magnet items are placed in awkward spots (such as information monitors being placed in narrow hallways where people can't stop to watch them without impeding foot traffic), there is at least a mixed message about whether these are meant to be social integrators or are just being put in leftover locations not good for anything else. This is, in fact, a pretty good barometer used by the troops to tell whether the new effort is serious or just a fad: are they allocated resources and locations that are a good design for the purpose, or are they given leftover space that is expedient? People can smell expediency like a dead fish in the wastebasket.

- In settings where the work is stressful and high pressured, are there spots in the workplace for personal regeneration? By this we mean places for people to get out of the main current for a bit, to withdraw and let their batteries recharge. When leaders espouse the importance of people remaining healthy on the job and being able to monitor and maintain their health through exercise, pacing, managing stress levels, and having satisfactory relationships with those around them, this should be backed up with some specific provisions for doing just that: exercise facilities or changing rooms for runners, quiet spaces that anyone can use (especially those who don't have a private office to hole up in), relatively quiet sitting areas for two or three people, and outdoor spaces if the weather permits their use. In one organization that provided a series of small lounges with a sofa, two chairs, and a coffee table, people use them all day long for various activities, some social and some private. They don't camp in them all day, as some prophesied, but rather use them as the need arises, and they have been very appreciative of the fact that they are there.

In sum, leaders need to be well aware of the under-the-surface message value of their choices about space design and use policies. New directions and change efforts can be strongly reinforced by workplace decisions that support the new directions. But these efforts can also be watered down or neutralized altogether by failing to provide the kinds of facilities and use patterns that would really support new focuses and ways of working.

Another key message function of the setting is to intentionally provide information about the place itself to users and visitors. Some of the more obvious messages include where different areas or groups are located, and how to reach them; the identity of the organization as a whole and of the parts; explicit behaviors that are or are not expected from people who are using or passing through a particular area; and what's going to happen in a process that a person is going through in that particular location.

GETTING AROUND

The model that we think of for designing a workplace that helps people know how to get around and what they should do in different places is the Walt Disney organization. At all their theme parks, the Disney people do an extremely careful job of designing the physical setting, the social contacts, and the signage experienced by users of any of the activities, displays, or rides. At attractions that are likely to have long lines, there are very clear instructions about where and when to get tickets, how long the estimated waiting time is (given the current length of the line), and other attractions (such as slide shows) to make the wait something more than just dead time. People are very aware of the thoughtfulness that is exhibited in such attention to detail, and that's part of what they remember and tell to others about their visit. It is also one of the things that keeps them coming back. The success of Disney's installations is built on the wallets of repeat customers.

This example illustrates how attention to such details communicates a thoughtfulness and caring about people's experiences. Well-presented place information is created by putting yourself into the place of the potential visitor or user: how did you get there, what would you be feeling and looking for as a result, what information would be helpful, and in what order, and what are you likely to be confused about? Following this line of reasoning through provides useful information at crucial points in the process. Not doing it also communicates information to the users: you didn't care enough to pay attention to the experience. Or, worse, people feel that the message is "you shouldn't be here in the first place."

For example, we used to visit an organization that had an almost hidden main entrance and no clear indication of where visitors should park. It turned out that there was a sign, but it was stuck in the ground at such an angle that no one could see it from the car. You could see the sign only after having parked and started searching for a door to enter. The feeling we always had was that the people who designed that place didn't really want visitors to come there.

The setting can provide information about what's what and what's where in a variety of ways. The most straightforward is some sort of signage that directs people to a menu of choices. The signage has to be placed in an easily findable spot, not like a building directory we once saw that was on a side wall around the corner from the entrance door. It was not visible to people who came in through the entrance door, and there was no reason to go around the corner, since it was not in the direction of the elevators. The maintenance worker who manned the lobby always marveled at how many dumb questions visitors asked and how stupid people seemed to be. It was a small miracle how much smarter people became when the directory was relocated to an immediately visible position.

Another way to provide information quickly is to make spaces more transparent, so that people can actually see where they are trying to go. Glass walls help, as do the internal atria that have become so popular in many corporate headquarters. The intent may be to create some sense of awe and grandeur, but a more useful immediate effect is to help people get a sense of the whole and roughly where things are located, so that they can orient themselves as they move around the building or complex.

SETTING EXPECTATIONS

Expectations about what people should do in an area can most straightforwardly be communicated by signage: NO SMOKING; KEEP RIGHT; EMPLOYEES ONLY; and so on. If these are relatively clear, people feel they have some sense of boundaries, and they usually respond well to this. It also takes employees out of the role of always having to tell violators that they are not living up to the code. If the code is not posted somewhere, people will inadvertently violate it, and members will be forced into a policing role, which they usually dislike.

Other ways of communicating behavioral expectations use physical layouts of spaces, such as dividers and other sorts of boundaries to stop movement (locked doors, card-access areas, dead-end corridors to discourage foot traffic, and the like). Often these are intentional, but sometimes they are not. We know many organizations where groups that are located next to each other, and who management would like to have working together, almost never see or talk to each other because the work station panels make communication such a deliberate, conscious effort. Removing or lowering the panels creates opportunity for eye contact and creates the expectation that communication is not merely possible but desirable.

The other part of helping to form expectations is informing people of what's going to happen when they come into a new setting. For instance, in a hospital admissions area this is done by informing outpatients about what the procedure will be when they come to a walk-in clinic. There is still a design element in this process, however, since the entrance should be obvious to the person arriving, and once inside, this person should be visible to someone at the clinic who can then inform them about what's going to happen.

We are not implying here that as the leader of an organization you have to wander all over the place making sure that all experiences by visitors and employees are consciously designed to be helpful and positive. But we do think that it is part of your role to make sure that such tests are performed. You should instill a sense of caring in those who do make such choices, so that the message of caring comes across as a matter of course.

A Sense of History

We want to close with consideration of one other aspect of organizational ecology in which communication processes are tied to work settings: the information that people read about history in the setting. One type of historic message is concerned with events that actually happened in that location. Organizational members see particular spots or arrangements and are reminded of events that they experienced there. They also have been told stories as part of the lore of the system, so that they associate particular spots with famous moments. "That's the conference room where Smithers told the chairman that we were going to be late and over budget on our DOD contract. Nobody ever does that anymore—we just let them find out however they can."

In this area, history is definitely in the eye of the beholder. One person simply sees desks, chairs, and decoration, while another sees and feels many ghosts of feelings and events from the past. They don't have to be legendary, just memorable for the person who is experiencing the flashback. This sense of history is part of the glue that holds the organizational community together, creating an experience of identification with the organization and one's own history and career.

For this reason, it is not a small decision when leaders decide to move from a traditional long-term location to a brand-new site. The obvious advantage is that you can make a workplace that fits tomorrow's demands and work style. The disadvantage is that you are also abandoning the identification, memories, and message value that adhere to the old setting. We are not talking about simple resistance to change here, although it often gets interpreted as that when people question whether the old place should be abandoned for greener pastures. What is at stake is the real, cumulative effect of the memories that people associate with the old location. The diagnostic question is whether there is more to be gained by moving (breaking old assumptions and attitudes, changing a culture that has outlived its usefulness) or by staying put and building on the sense of community provided by the messages in the place.

To give an example, the history of Digital Equipment Corporation has been very closely linked to the large mill complex in which it was founded in Maynard, Massachusetts. The company began by renting space in one small corner of the mill. Over the years it gradually occupied the whole collection of buildings, not to mention many other buildings around the world. And yet, there remains an aura about the mill itself, an almost palpable climate of "this is where it all began." People have often refused to move out of the mill into "better" quarters, or have jockeyed to move into it when space became available.

Part of this draw can be attributed to the fact that the CEO and key corporate staff have continued to be located in the mill, so it is seen as a visible power center. But many people have described the general aura of the place as going beyond this, encompassing a feel for the whole history of the company. The inconveniences (such as spiders dropping from the ceiling into coffee cups) are seen as symbolic of the frontier spirit and experiences of the early days—something that people want very much to hold on to. People care more about having this gutsy feel to their work life than they do about having slicker, more modern conveniences. This has changed recently, probably in part due to the invited departure of DEC's founder, Ken Olson. The company is trying to reinvent itself, and along with many other changes, the mill is now up for sale, in a sense underscoring the importance it has played in the company's culture to this point.

Sometimes company leaders are much more explicit about creating work settings that communicate the history of the enterprise. In particular, graphics, photographs, products, famous members of the organization, and the like can be displayed in ways that give people a real feel for who these people were and what life was like in the organization in the past. For example, the lobby of the Decker Engineering building at Corning Glass features a very well-done display of products and scientific processes that have shaped the company's development. Although the building itself is not old, a visitor feels very connected with the history of Corning after looking at the exhibit. It also helps that the displays are located in a way that provides a natural progression in time and makes it very easy to follow while waiting for your host to come to the lobby.

It All Counts

It's a fact of life that workplace designs are read by users and visitors for information of several kinds, including identity, intentions, expectations, status, history, and the like. Too often, the importance of these kinds of environmental messages is overlooked or underemphasized. And when conscious attention is paid by the organizational leaders, it tends to focus on the highly visible aspects of the building: its facade, reception area, dining room, executive conference rooms. These areas deserve attention. Our intention is simply to broaden the range of issues considered when planning, designing, and managing workplaces so that there is an increased likelihood of creating not simply a clear statement about image, but a high-performance workplace that reinforces desired ways of working through all its environmental messages. This requires not allocating too many of the scarce environmental resources to supporting status distinctions. These tend to build in many hidden constraints and rigidities that block or retard productive behavior and changes. The old answer, "status symbols help people know where they stand," represents a very marginal return on a major investment. Such information should be communicated in more direct and cheaper ways.

CHAPTER FOUR

Designing to Accommodate Change

Change is endemic in today's organizations. Asking for an organizational chart is more likely to elicit chuckles than an actual piece of paper. Before the ink is dry on one organizational structure, senior management often has moved on to another. In a new building project, plans showing which groups sit in which part of the building become obsolete several times before any group occupies the space. Just when work surfaces are expanded to accommodate new and larger computers, the computers become smaller. But then the prices on peripherals like printers drop, so more and more work stations are fitted out with them, which means more work surface is needed again. And the workers themselves are changing: there are more older workers, dual-income families, women, and ethnic groups. Their different work styles and lifestyles are rapidly making much of the homogeneity of corporate America a historical curiosity.

Another generator of change is the increasing concern about environmental quality, led by states such as California that are creating governmental pressures to reduce the number of commuters and the length of their journeys. The negative consequences are not all environmental. In interviews done as part of a study of telework by Cornell University's International Workplace Studies Program (Becker, Rappaport, Quinn, and Sims, 1993), employees in Palmdale, a sprawling bedroom community about an hour and a half east of Los Angeles, talked about Palmdale's high rate of child abuse. The pattern of parents leaving for work at 5:30 A.M. and returning, exhausted, at 7:00 P.M. appeared to be a contributing factor.

While all this is going on, many organizations are trying to reengineer their basic business processes and instill a new culture that emphasizes teamwork, seeks to flatten the organizational hierarchy, and empowers staff. Oh, yes . . . and reduce costs.

All this change can seem, and often is, overwhelming. It is a bit like getting married, moving, and taking on a new job all at the same time. The individual and organizational stress that accumulates under such conditions can sap energy and divert attention to the point where it becomes dysfunctional.

Planning for and managing this kind of change is another facet of what organizational ecology is all about. Organizations, like any other dynamic ecosystem, continuously make adaptations in response to changing internal and external conditions. They must, in order to stay alive and promote healthy development over time. This chapter looks at the relation between change in organizational characteristics such as size, structure, and information technology and the ecology of the workplace.

Pressures for Change

Pressures for change come from many sources. The demographics of the workforce itself are changing. White males are being joined by more women and minorities. Nuclear families with children and both parents present have become a relative rarity, while the proportion of single parent families has risen significantly. Concern for teamwork and flatter organizational hierarchies are redefining the kinds of skills that are needed to manage effectively. Global markets and tough competition have forced companies to drive costs down, in the process leading them to consider outsourcing of noncore functions. Outsourcing transforms the nature of the bond between employee and corporation. And then there is the profusion of new information technologies that promise to make work easier, faster, and cheaper, but sometimes simply overwhelm us. It is within this context of change that a new workscape is emerging.

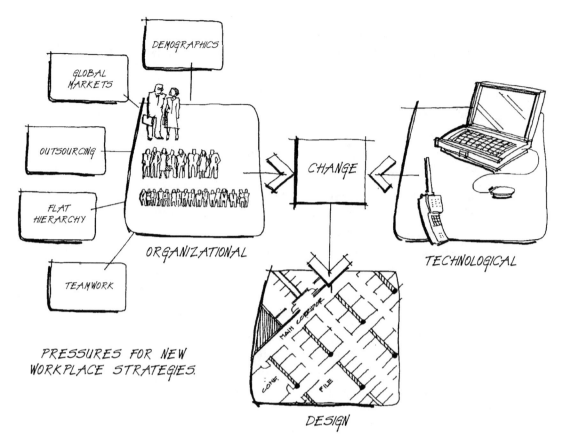

GLOBAL MARKETS

DEMOGRAPHICS

OUTSOURCING

FLAT HIERARCHY

TEAMWORK

ORGANIZATIONAL

CHANGE

TECHNOLOGICAL

DESIGN

PRESSURES FOR NEW WORKPLACE STRATEGIES.

ORGANIZATIONAL CHANGE

To reduce costs, companies like IBM have not only reduced the overall size of their organization dramatically; they have also redistributed people from administrative functions (cost centers) to sales functions (revenue generators). Part of the streamlining and reorganization occurring in all sorts of companies involves decisions to combine departments and divisions; for example, having the human resources and finance groups or the facilities and real estate departments reporting to a single vice president. The intent is to improve communication and integration among related functions, and to simplify and speed up decision making. For much the same reasons, in manufacturing organizations such as Ford, Toyota, Chrysler, and DuPont, to name a few, research and development staff that once occupied different buildings are being brought together under one roof or on one campus.

From an organizational ecology perspective, the issue is not only which groups should work together and be part of the same team, but

how the design of the *places* where they work can support the new business processes being put into place. A major dilemma facing such
dynamic organizations is how to accommodate these kinds of organizational changes with the minimum amount of disturbance to the work
process and at the lowest possible cost.

CHANGE IN INFORMATION TECHNOLOGY

Change that has implications for the ecology of the workplace occurs not
just in business processes and organizational size and structure, but also
in the nature of the information technology that simultaneously supports
and often stimulates changes in these organizational characteristics.

The equipment that sits on our desks is shrinking rapidly. There are
now laptop and notebook computers smaller than a sheet of paper and
weighing four to six pounds or less—and they are likely to shrink in size
and weight drastically in the next two to three years. But there are also
more items of peripheral equipment sitting on our desks. Many notebook computers, for instance, plug into a desktop docking system so that
when working in the office a person can use a larger screen that is easier
to read. But as the display technology continues to improve on the note-
books, it is likely that fewer people will expect to work on a large screen
except for special applications, such as desktop publishing or working
with CAD systems, so the larger monitors may disappear altogether, or
take the form of flat screens hung on walls rather than sitting on the desk.

While the size of information technology equipment is undoubtedly
decreasing, the functional variety of this technology is growing rapidly.
Some of these technologies are: high-speed fax transmission, desktop
video, multimedia programs that allow full integration of text, voice,
graphics, sound, and video; cordless and cellular telephones; computers
that answer telephone calls; telephones whose number is attached to a
person, not a place; sophisticated pagers that send and receive text messages; increasing use of CD-ROMS that store immense amounts of
information; access to worldwide data bases and networks such as the
Internet. The list is long and requires updating continuously.

What all this technology means is that people can now access information and contact other people almost anywhere in the world. Lotus
Development Corporation is planning a new corporate headquarters

using a variety of consultants and project managers who are linked and communicate primarily through LotusNotes, a groupware computer program they developed. Price-Waterhouse, Andersen Consulting, and many other companies are using the same program to generate proposals, using people working in places as far-flung as Australia, London, and New York. These kinds of information technologies have ecological as well as organizational implications.

Responding to Change

Initially, the most sensible way of responding to these changes seemed to be to create an environment as flexible as the organization occupying it. With the explosion of integrated panel-based furniture systems throughout the 1970s and 80s, this flexibility typically took the form of furniture that could be reconfigured and reused when change occurred, rather than having to tear down and rebuild walls. The problem, some organizations found, was that the easy flexibility encouraged change, and while the panel-based furniture systems were designed to be reconfigured, doing so still disrupted work operations. Space standards that used work station size to reflect and reward rank further complicated the situation. Slowly, organizations began to look for new solutions to workplace flexibility.

ONE SIZE FITS ALL

The previous chapter briefly described Union Carbide and Aetna Life and Casualty's "universal plan" offices. The concept is extremely simple: designed carefully, a single structure can accommodate considerable diversity. We experience the principle of a universal plan every day. Think of bookshelves. The same bookshelf accommodates books of different height, thickness, and width. One size may not fit all, but it is likely to fit 90 percent of the books we have. The same is true of parking spaces: a motorcycle, monster truck, sports car, or family sedan can fit into the same size parking space. For a single size that fits an even wider range of elements, think of a coat hanger: the same structure accommodates women's, children's, and men's clothes: shirts, trousers, jackets, coats, in any color, any length, any style.

The same principle applies in the office context. The one-size office allows considerable variation within the footprint in terms of the type and layout of furnishings provided, and thus the kind of work and work style it supports. In its pure form, which rarely occurs in the workplace, this would mean every single office in a building would be the same size (hence, universal).

In practice, most organizations use a variation of the universal plan that limits the number of different office sizes. In a three-level system, one office size accommodates about 80 percent or more of the support, professional, and lower-level management staff. Another office size, accounting for about 15 percent of the total, would be for senior managers, all occupying the same size manager's office. The remaining 5 percent, typically representing only a few offices, would be occupied by the most senior executives, people like the chairman, the president, and the executive vice presidents. This approach is applicable across industry types and organizations of different sizes.

Universal plan offices represent not so much a total reduction in the amount of space required as a redistribution of the available space. The offices of the most senior people tend to shrink, while those of the most junior people tend to expand. The benefit in comparison to the more traditional highly differentiated space-by-rank approach to allocating corporate property is much greater flexibility. The consequence of this flexibility is fewer barriers to reorganization, less disruption when it occurs, and lower costs in money and time. Managers at Aetna estimate that adopting the universal plan offices reduced the costs of churn in their organization in excess of $300,000 annually.

What goes into the universal footprint and how it is managed vary considerably. At Aetna, for example, all the furniture used within a given size footprint is part of the same furniture system. Variation occurs in which particular components are used. Someone in the facilities group may have a drafting table, while someone in accounting has a conventional work surface. Some people may prefer more overhead shelves, others more storage bins. A short person may have a footstool; a person doing a lot of computer data entry gets a wrist support shelf. Everyone would have an adjustable keyboard shelf and task lighting. The components used depend on job function and work style, and also on personal and physical differences.

In Scandinavian companies, where this type of universal plan office is very common, the person occupying the office simply calls a number to ask for more bookshelves or an extra file cabinet. As long as the items can fit safely within the office, they are delivered promptly. Equity results from everyone being able to have the furniture and equipment they need to get their job done, not from everyone having exactly the same thing because they happen to be the same rank or do the same job.

THE FIXED SERVICE SPINE

In companies like Aetna, the universal plan is integrated with another concept that combines rigidity with flexibility. It is the concept of a fixed service spine. What this means, simply, is that all the hard-wired services, such as power and data and voice lines, are located in a fixed grid pattern. These design elements are expensive to install and move; hence the decision to locate them once and only once.

The lines of the grid constitute the spine. It is the fixed element. From this fixed spine are "hung" the standard module offices that make up the universal plan office. The flexibility comes from the opportunity to easily, quickly, and with minimal disruption reconfigure the panels hanging perpendicular to the spine. Thus, rather than having two people in two separate offices, a team office for two people can almost instantaneously be created by removing one panel. If the organization wants to have teams of four, other team members can

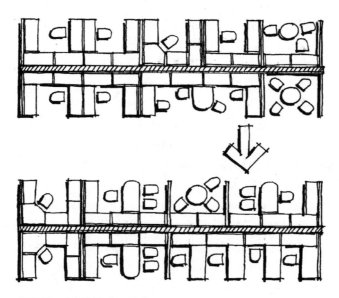

FIXED SERVICE SPINE

be located in the facing spine. Variations in what kinds of tables, equipment, display, or storage areas the team or individuals need can be accommodated in the space between the two facing spines by varying the nature of the furniture and equipment there, all without undermining the value of the rigid backbone around which all the variation occurs.

These kinds of principles illustrate how careful attention to the planning, design, and management of the workplace as a physical setting can contribute to the organization's ability to continually update how it works. This is quite a departure from workplaces that dictate organizational behaviors by making it so difficult, expensive, or time-consuming and disruptive to manipulate the environment that the decision is made, consciously, to have people continue working in dysfunctional ways.

TIGHT- VERSUS LOOSE-FIT DESIGN

If it is true that we cannot predict accurately how many pieces of technology will be in the office (or briefcase) or what size and configuration they will be, then the least effective office design is what we could call "tight-fit" design. This is the kind of design in which, for example, an overhead projector is fitted precisely into a hole in a conference table so that it can be dropped from sight when not in use. Sounds great, and it is—until the projector size becomes one inch larger, or smaller, or has a different shape. Then the table becomes useless.

Tight fit/Loose fit

More useful in the face of uncertainty is a "loose-fit" approach to design. Here the idea is that the same table or room could accommodate many different pieces of equipment, of different sizes and shapes, over time. It suggests erring on the large size, and developing a universal size, as noted earlier, that can accommodate different uses. At Union Carbide, for example, the same size office module was designed to be used for a one-person office, a two-person office, a conference room with conference table, or an informal meeting area. Free-standing furniture that can be easily reconfigured by those using it is, from this perspective, a loose-fit approach, and it is likely to better accommodate unpredictable change—like that which occurs in a

TIGHT FIT

LOOSE FIT

team-oriented environment—than furniture that is part of a fixed interlocking system. Conference tables made up of rearrangeable pieces are much more functional than a single monolithic slab that cannot be reshaped.

THE REAL ESTATE PORTFOLIO

A similar loose-fit approach can also be applied to the organization's overall real estate portfolio. Combining everyone under a single roof, or on a single floor, is a major objective for many companies. It is the driving force behind the gigantic buildings and huge floorplates (the size of a basic floor) we see in cities everywhere. Part of the goal is a desire for efficiency: having everyone in a single building can reduce the duplication of services and the number of people required to provide and maintain them. Creating large centers of activity also helps justify the purchase of more expensive and specialized equipment. It is exactly the same justification used for building large "magnet" schools. Part of the goal is also organizational: having more people in the same place is presumed to foster communication and build a sense of cohesiveness that cuts across subgroups, departmental and division lines, and disciplines.

There is good reason to question some of these assumptions about "big is better." Magnet schools have not demonstrated that they improve the learning and proficiency levels of students, and many large high schools are looking for ways to create some form of "house" system that divides the school into smaller units that foster a stronger sense of being part of a meaningful group. Research by psychologists Roger Barker and Paul Gump (1964) has also shown that in large high schools students tend to be less involved in the school's activities and take less of a leadership role. In the workplace there are similar kinds of evidence suggesting that in terms of job satisfaction and organizational commitment, "small is better."

This does not mean organizations should be small, but as General Electric's CEO Jack Welch likes to say, he wants GE to be a big company that acts like a small one. The new information technologies mentioned above make that kind of small feeling more possible. People can work from their homes, from satellite offices and telework centers, from airports and airline clubs, from hotels and automobiles far more easily than they could just a few years ago.

One implication for organizations, many of whom have worked very hard to consolidate as many people into as few buildings or floors as possible, is that physical decentralization may make a lot of sense. This should not be taken to mean all employees working by themselves, in isolation. It simply means being open to fresh ideas, such as taking a short-term lease in a building that offers fully furnished office suites for employees who live near each other; or banding together with other companies and putting surplus space into a common data base to create a kind of "office club" in which people can use any of the specially designated space in any of the participating companies' buildings whenever it is convenient to do so.

The key point is that the range of spaces, in terms of size, character, ownership, and location, considered part of the workplace portfolio are likely to increase, in part because new information technologies make it so much easier to work from anywhere at any time (hence, the term "the virtual office"), and because this kind of workplace ecology responds positively to a number of challenges organizations are facing. These include increasing concern among employees about the quality of their lives, and especially their work/family relationships; the need for companies to be able to maintain mobility and flexibility in the face of rapidly changing and unpredictable shifts in market conditions; the need to attract a very high-quality workforce that is more diverse in terms of age, ethnicity, work style, and lifestyle than ever before; the need to meet new and more stringent state and federal regulations concerning air quality and traffic congestion (and hence commuting); and the desire to be closer to customers.

ENVIRONMENTAL MISMATCHES

While the different ways of accommodating change do have an impact on the culture of an organization, for the most part their primary purpose is not to change or challenge the culture. Universal plan offices, for example, do undermine conventional status systems, but their primary purpose is to reduce the cost and disruption associated with organizational churn by making it possible to move people without having to move walls or panels. The planning and design of the workplace can, however, be used—or serve—as a deliberate catalyst for organizational change, including the culture of the organization. It is hard to understand the impact of a workplace on an organization without understanding the role that an organization's culture plays in the design and use of the workplace.

When we use the term "organizational culture," we refer to a number of elements in a particular organization: expectations and assumptions about how good members should behave; common language and understanding about the meaning of words and events; major policies; symbolic meanings assigned to the design and use of space; the look and feel of the organization and its members; basic assumptions about the way the world works; and commonly held values about what is worth doing and how it should be done.

The work setting is sometimes used as a tool to encourage culture change. By changing layouts and technology, you make it easier to work in certain ways and more difficult to work in others, thereby influencing patterns of behavior over time. In some instances this will affect the norms and expectations that people apply to one another. A new facility project can also be a spur to helping an organization's leaders assess their culture and make choices about which aspects to keep and which to try to change. If it is done thoughtfully, making decisions about project goals and design criteria should result in a clarification of the system's goals, values, and key success factors, including which ones need to change for future survival.

All of these influences become most visible when there is a mismatch between the organization's culture and the structure or feel of its facilities. There are three interesting types: the unintentional mismatch, the intentional mismatch, and the transitional mismatch.

The Unintentional Mismatch

The link between facilities and organizational culture becomes painfully obvious when a company moves to a new setting that is inconsistent with its culture and style. This usually happens when the place was planned using mainly quantitative criteria: how many people accommodated, how many square feet, how much equipment and cabling capacity, and so on. There may also have been image considerations, such as how it was supposed to look to visitors, but usually not enough attention was paid to the "feel" of the company: how people relate to each other, how work gets done, what the time expectations are, where events should happen, and who should be able to see whom easily.

For example, Levi Strauss outgrew its San Francisco headquarters in the early 1970s and decided to move to several floors of a new high-rise office tower nearby. Very soon after moving, people began to feel that the new space did not fit their informal cultural style. Executives now used a different bank of elevators because of the floors they were on. There was no common lobby to serve as gathering space. As a *Fortune* writer noted, "Lower-ranking employees missed what Howard Friedman, Levi's chief consulting architect, calls the old Levi spirit: 'Good morning, how's the baby?' The interiors were so white, so cold-blooded that they seemed almost sterile" (Breckenfield, 1982, p. 112).

After considerable soul searching, the company's leaders began an expensive and demanding process of creating a new headquarters in a low-rise mix of old renovated warehouses and new structures clustered around an outdoor space they renamed Levi Plaza. "'We belong down on the ground, no higher than treetop level,' explained Executive Vice President Robert D. Haas. 'This is the kind of company we've been, and should get back to'" (Breckenfield, 1982, p. 110).

In other words, they felt that the mismatch between their corporate culture and the new headquarters was creating a serious risk of losing both their sense of identity and valued employees, who were becoming increasingly dissatisfied with the feel of their new, more sterile workplace. The leaders decided it was worth the money and trouble to try it again, creating a more appropriate setting that matched a highly valued culture. In the process they also made a new urban place that has reinforced a strong sense of public identity for the company.

The Intentional Mismatch

There are times when an organization's leaders will deliberately choose to create a new work setting that does *not* reflect the current culture and style of the organization. They do this when they are trying to transform the system in ways that will help it function better in a changed or changing environment. The leaders have generally examined their mission, compared their needed culture with the actual one, and defined some directions for cultural change. As one means to this end, they have identified new ways of working that they want to encourage, along with workplace design criteria to support the new style.

If they make a physical change and hope for the best, the effort is likely to have the same disquieting effects as the unintentional mismatch just described. They also need to design a parallel process to go with the physical change, dealing with cultural change to match the vision of the future company.

This process is aimed at education and behavioral change so that changes in the setting aren't treated simply as odd mistakes to be neutralized by doing business in the same old ways. The approach is illustrated by a recent renovation of a Boston-based firm called Work/Family Directions. Over the past decade Work/Family Directions has become the leader in providing employees of Fortune 500 companies with a range of counseling and information services intended to help employees reduce stress related to conflicting demands of family and work life. Employees whose company subscribes to Work/Family Directions services, for example, can get help concerning their children's progress at school, childcare options, or their elderly parents' health and housing needs. They get the help in two basic forms: through direct telephone counseling with professional staff located in Boston, and through specialized publications about the issues for which the employee has asked for help.

Before the renovation, all counseling staff occupied identical work stations, eight feet by eight feet. With the exception of a few small meeting areas in corridors, and a few schedulable conference rooms, there was no other place to conduct the telephone interviews, which can be stressful, or to meet informally with other counselors to discuss the kinds of issues that arise in the counseling sessions. Because basically the only workspace was the work cubicle, there was no place, other than in corridors or conference rooms or standing in a cubicle, to share information about new resources, services, research findings, and so on, and to do one's own research, all of which are critical to providing customers with high-quality service. Dedicated counselors expended the energy needed to compensate for the constraining environment. But Work/Family Directions co-owner Charles Rodgers wanted an environment that enhanced performance and made the company the best place possible to work.

Through a series of interactive workshops, a new design was developed that radically changed how the counselors worked. To provide more privacy and a better environment for concentrating while working with clients on the telephone, a series of "sanctuaries" was built, located on a mezzanine floor, away from the bustle of the first floor. Counselors now use these unassigned, nonterritorial work stations when they are on call, but when they are off duty they now have a wide array of places, all with a distinct character, where they can choose to work: an open space along a wall of windows; a variety of comfortable and "homelike" furniture; an oblong, amoeba-shaped table near a beverage area that is outfitted with computers so people can relax with a cup of coffee while looking at e-mail, chatting with someone, or just reading a book or report. There are two different conference areas that do not have to be scheduled, and other unassigned work stations that anyone can use.

The environment is radically different, as is the way of working. The goal was to create an intentional mismatch with the previous way of assigning space and performing different facets of the work that would enhance performance, reduce stress, and promote more effective teamwork and collaboration.

Transitional Mismatches

In the case of a transitional mismatch, the new work setting does not reflect the organization's old culture, but it accidentally fits with what the culture (in flux) is becoming. The physical change helps to speed up the change by helping employees work in new ways and by making them more aware of their preferences for the new culture and ways of working.

For example, a small business firm, approximately a hundred employees, moved into a larger workspace on the Boston waterfront. The offices the company took over had been created by a stock brokerage firm, and all offices and other rooms on the window walls had full glass fronts to get daylight and the great views of the harbor into the interior of the space. The new occupants said, "We can't work this way—it's like being on display all the time." They resolved to hang drapes until they could build solid walls to replace the glass office fronts, but time and cost considerations led them to live with it as it was for a while.

Interesting things began to happen after they moved in. People could find each other without having to ask secretaries or the receptionist—they could see who was where. When a key event happened in their fast-paced global business, everyone knew about it in a very short time: they could see an air of excitement in the way people were conversing, so they knew to ask what was happening. Meetings in the glass-fronted conference room became more energetic, and visual displays were left up to be read by anyone who was interested. There were many fewer secrets, and a general increase in openness was felt in the way people communicated day to day.

The upshot is that they never put up the drapes, and they certainly didn't replace the glass with solid walls. The visual openness struck a real chord with them. They both liked it and needed it because of the demands of their business, although it had not been consciously recognized until they lived in and experienced the new setting that more or less demanded such behavior.

The point is simply that there are a number of ways to look at the mutual influence between corporate culture and physical facilities. Mismatches can cause problems if they are accidental and inappropriate; or they can be a useful tool for change if the new setting is consistent with directions in which the organization's culture is changing or needs to change.

As the examples of Levi Strauss and the other companies suggest, facilities planning cannot be treated as an end in itself. It must always be grounded in consideration of business goals and organizational culture, both in the present and with respect to long-term change directions.

Both the workplace design and the space management process should be consistent with the goals and culture, or people will feel continually unsupported and ill served by their workplace.

In terms of the overall theme of this chapter, the directions for culture change should be consistent with those we see as necessary for workplace design: toward a more flexible, less static way of working that can be shaped and reshaped by the members as they go. The facilities should make it easy to do this without costly renovations and even costlier time delays in getting on with the work. The culture and management processes should both expect and encourage people to take advantage of that flexibility.

CHAPTER FIVE

Making Space for Teamwork

What first grabs the attention at the Hexcel Corporation's new corporate headquarters in Pleasanton, California, are the basketball shoes: size 22 extra wide. The shoes and the other sports equipment on display in the lobby are made from strong and lightweight honeycomb materials. Depending on the material used, honeycomb can become the highly flexible and spongy sole of a high-technology basketball shoe or the rigid material used in the construction of Boeing aircraft. Hexcel Corporation is a worldwide leader in the development and manufacture of honeycomb materials and reinforced fabrics, advanced composites, and resins.

The problem is that Hexcel's large aerospace customer base is facing difficult times. To survive as a company Hexcel must find new markets and discover new applications for honeycomb. Products such as composite baseball bats and inserts for Reebok shoes reflect the changing times.

Hexcel's senior management realized that inventing new markets required new thinking about how the organization functioned, and in particular how the different divisions within the corporate headquarters office related to and communicated with each other. The original three-story corporate headquarters building isolated the different business units. There was no center. Each floor had its own drab break room, and the executives were located together in closed offices on the perimeter of the third floor. The majority of professional and support staff sat in work stations away from the windows.

The overall effect was visually uniform and dull. Many staff members felt that they did not know what was going on in the company as a whole. This was a major disadvantage at a time when the company leaders felt that they needed to break down barriers and improve communication between internal groups so that, for example, Hexcel could sell products from different divisions to the same customer.

At the time the possibility of a new headquarters was suggested, these kinds of organizational challenges were facing Hexcel, but they were originally not part of the brief. What triggered the decision to move the headquarters to a vacant building about ten miles from its existing location was pure real estate economics. By moving, Hexcel expected over the next ten years to save roughly $250,000 annually in rent, with lower operating expenses contributing an additional $100,000 per year in savings.

What transformed a sensible real estate decision weakly linked to helping the company address its fundamental business concerns to a decision that made both financial and organizational sense was project manager Alan Drake's interest in organizational ecology. Drake, a transplanted Scotsman, appreciated the need to reduce costs. But he also believed that the new building project had the potential to reflect and support organizational change without imposing radical change that would be resisted.

As Drake noted, "We chose to lease an existing structure in one of two major business parks some thirty-five miles east of San Francisco. The building, constructed in the mid-1980s, is a one-story, 55,000-square-foot rectangular structure of no great architectural interest." All existing interior improvements were demolished, leaving an open plan with two restroom cores.

The architect, John Holey, suggested the idea of an interior "Main Street" to link the two halves of the rectangle and to act as a main thoroughfare. He suggested two other elements that would emphasize this traffic pattern. One was to centralize support services—copy, travel arrangements, mail, refreshments, and a resource center—in a single magnet area, a kind of corporate town square that became known as the hub. The other was to place all the conference rooms along Main

Street, removing the problem of departmental ownership and providing additional reasons to use the street.

To reinforce the importance of groups as well as individuals, small, user-defined areas called pavilions were provided in different quadrants of the building; staff members from the same business unit, and from different business units, used the pavilions for a variety of purposes. In Drake's words, "More open space, while clearly beneficial, also has the potential to create a mass of work stations with little definition." The pavilions address this issue: the areas are framed by centralized filing cabinets and a large skylight above. Counters above the filing can accommodate a variety of support needs including printers, fax machines, and small copiers. Lounge seating below the skylight provides an opportunity for informal meetings.

No formal post-occupancy study has been completed yet, but the preliminary informal feedback is extremely positive, especially given a difficult financial year and an uncertain future. Employees have expressed pleasure at the open atmosphere, window locations, skylights, natural light, and large functional work stations. There is a much greater sense of the energy of the organization. Activity in offices, in conference rooms, along the Main Street, and Town Center is much easier to see. Senior managers are more visible and less anonymous.

"The more informal work settings," according to Drake, "were slower to gain employee approval. In the beginning the dining area, resource center, and pavilions were little used. They were foreign to the recent work experience of most employees. However, as those people with a sense of drama or adventure began to use the spaces it became acceptable to be found reading in the resource center or talking on Main Street." The definition of "real work" is also beginning to change, and communication is increasing as a result.

As skeptics at Hexcel have pointed out, "people, not buildings, change the direction of a company." That is true, but a facility and the process for planning and designing it can encourage and support such change. Drake argues that "moving the corporate headquarters saved Hexcel money at a time when it needed to save money but, perhaps of equal importance, it provided tangible evidence of the new start and management's commitment to change." In the overall scheme of things the kinds of changes made at Hexcel are not radical, and by themselves they will not make Hexcel a better or more competitive organization. But they are meaningful, and that is why they provide useful lessons for other organizations.

Redefining "Real Work"

Organizational leaders today face a major challenge in creating work settings that promote creativity and innovation. When companies are faced with no alternative but to use fewer resources to become more productive, all organizational members—from executives to support staff—need to be encouraged to break out of old assumptions and abandon solutions that have outlived their usefulness. For many executives a key ingredient is changing entrenched ideas about teamwork, and that means significantly expanding the concept of what kinds of communication are useful and, ultimately, what gets thought of as "real work."

Led by efficiency experts over the past seventy-five years, many companies began to see informal communication as synonymous with socializing, and that meant wasting time. Talking was all right as long as it occurred as part of a scheduled meeting. There, it could drone on for hours and still be real work, while a five-minute conversation at the water cooler or in the corridor was considered to be "time out." Efficiency became defined as focusing directly on the task, whatever it was: typing, telephoning, writing a report, reading a memo, or participating in a scheduled meeting.

This stance also reflected the view that the individual is the key ingredient to productivity, rather than the team or group, and that competition among individuals and groups is preferable to cooperation because it "motivates" people. This view was personified by the adage that "a camel is a horse designed by a committee." This perception of "real work" simply ignores the fact that long cycles of product development or products and services that don't meet customer expectations are a major price for poor coordination and "chimney" organizational units that make a point of not sharing information, plans, and experience across departmental lines.

Problems in today's world—whether in the computer, automobile, pharmaceutical, insurance, or other industries—are much more complex, and the expertise needed to resolve them is more diverse. One person does not build a car, a computer, a new insurance program, a telephone switch, or a benefits package. Solving these problems requires expertise and experience that cross disciplinary and departmental boundaries. In this context, teamwork, communication, and collaboration not only are not wasted time, they are fundamental building blocks to organizational effectiveness.

It is for these kinds of reasons that companies such as Chrysler and Ford have reengineered their product development process. Design departments that only a few years ago occupied separate buildings, with locks on the doors to keep out not just the potential industrial spy but their own company's engineers, have been replaced with new development centers that are organized and designed around the principle of simultaneous engineering and platform teams. At Ford, for example, teams sitting in the same area now include people from marketing, engineering, purchasing, and design. They work together from the beginning of the product development cycle, rather than the old absurd system: they had to line up on special days to get a meeting pass into the design center for a peek at what the stylists were cooking up, designs they would eventually have to figure out how to manufacture in a cost-effective manner.

The old-style development process at Ford reminds us of a major American manufacturing company with which we worked several years ago. In its early days its products were so unique that its main problem was simply choosing who would receive them. Marketing and sales were basically a nonissue. That changed dramatically when Japanese companies started making similar products that were more reliable, cheaper, and had more features. The company came close to bankruptcy. At that point its senior management initiated a serious effort to build in total quality management throughout the company with a much greater emphasis on teamwork.

Yet as we looked around we saw no places, literally, for teams to meet. Individual offices were not designed to accommodate more than two to three people, at most, and there were only a couple of conference rooms per floor. These were in enormous demand, and yet did not function very well. They had to be scheduled well in advance; they had little free wall space and were therefore poorly equipped for capturing or displaying teamwork and team activities. Because the room was used

for different meetings throughout the day, as soon as one meeting ended, everything that might have been tacked or taped to walls or written on flipcharts or white boards had to be removed and team members disappeared in all directions to their own personal offices.

Out of sight, out of mind. No one could take a look at what had been produced in its original form, letting ideas sink in and new thoughts form; and the distance and isolation of individual offices meant discussions that might be generated by looking at materials together, or just having something come up while working on something else, rarely happened. At best, one had to make a deliberate effort to contact another team member, usually by telephone. If the material was copied for distribution, that often took days or weeks, during which time the project had already moved on. It was not an effective or an efficient way of working together as a team.

In response to these kinds of environments and the frustrating dysfunctions they engender, a number of companies are now creating high-performance workplaces that are designed specifically to support team-work and collaboration.

Communication and the Rugby Versus the Relay-Race Model

Creating high-performance workplaces in which the organizational structures and cultures promote easy communication and relationship building often is a part of a more general effort to move from a "relay-race" model of the product development cycle to a "rugby" model. In the relay-race model each function or discipline (marketing, for example) does its work and then tosses it over the fence to the next group (design), who is supposed to run with their part of the development process until it is finished, at which point they toss their output to the next group (engineering), and so on, until the finished product comes out the door. Unfortunately, what goes over the fence has a tendency to be thrown back, as work in later stages reveals problems with choices made in ear-lier stages. Like a neighbor whose yard serves as the outfield for the kids next door, it can tend to create hard feelings and harsh words. It's not a friendly process, and eats up time in reworking the problem.

The rugby model (it could easily be basketball, or hockey, or soccer) brings all the players in the process together as a team at the project's inception. Different players may take a stronger lead at different points in the process, and the ball will move all over the field, sometimes going backward or laterally to move forward, as the team moves it toward the goal. The whole team is in the game all the time, so that decisions in dif-ferent phases are known and tested for consistency and compatibility as they occur.

The glue that holds the team together is constant communication, some of it planned and some spontaneous and unplanned. It is not like American football, with its regular huddles and time outs. Communication in the rugby model is on the fly, in the halls, on the stairs, at lunch, in the locker room. In the relay-race model communication is in the conference room—planned, scheduled, predetermined.

The challenge, then, is how to configure buildings on a site, and areas within a building, to support the more dynamic rugby-model approach to the product development process. One example of how this has been done is Steelcase's Corporate Development Center (Becker, 1990), which also served as a model in many ways for Ford's new research and engineering center.

The Steelcase CDC

Steelcase, Inc., headquartered in Grand Rapids, Michigan, is the world's largest manufacturer of contract office furniture.* About six miles away from its corporate headquarters, in the center of a field on the outskirts of Grand Rapids, is the Corporate Development Center (CDC). Construction on the seven-level, 575,000-square-foot building began in May 1986 and was completed in May 1989. The building's design is intended to meet two major objectives: (1) to contribute to the development of more innovative products that will enable Steelcase to maintain its preeminent position in the furniture industry; (2) to significantly speed up the product development cycle so that new products can be brought to market faster, thereby responding better to shifts in the marketplace.

THE TOTAL WORKPLACE CONCEPT

Steelcase had a clear vision of both short-range goals and objectives, and the longer view of what the organization stands for and should do to prosper over the long haul. These values included the recognition of the basic worth of individuals; the need for the building to be as dynamic as the organization occupying it; and the value of effectiveness, which sometimes must be bought at the expense of simple efficiency.

These ideas came together in three different facets of the total workplace concept. One was the idea of integrating decisions often considered in isolation by individual departments, such as human resources, information technology, design and construction, and buildings operations and management. The second aspect was that the workplace is more than one's own personal office or work station. It is the entire workplace (site, amenities, commons areas, project rooms, support areas), a series of loosely coupled settings. The third was the idea that the processes used

*This case is excerpted from F. Becker, The Total Workplace: Facilities Management and the Elastic Corporation (New York: Van Nostrand Reinhold, 1990).

for planning, designing, and managing the workplace are as much a part of the building's quality as are its physical characteristics.

The fundamental structure of the CDC project was based on the rugby model, namely that innovative product solutions require enormous amounts of information about markets, technology, design, and the production process to be widely shared at all stages of the development process. Informal communication across project teams and across disciplines and departments to stimulate creativity was the bedrock of what Steelcase called the "advanced work culture." Its distinguishing features were its emphasis on teamwork that cuts across discipline and departmental boundaries; high value placed on free-flowing and serendipitous face-to-face communication; clear goals reached by mutual discussion, taking advantage of unexpected ideas and opportunities; and information and ideas moving among all players from the very beginning of the process, not in some rigid, preset sequence.

ORGANIZATIONAL PRINCIPLES

The rugby model's emphasis on informal communication made stimulating face-to-face interaction, especially serendipitous communication among groups such as product engineering, industrial design, and marketing, a key element in creating the design center. Steelcase's emphasis on informal communication was based in large part on the work of MIT professor Thomas Allen (1977). Allen's research shows that performance in R&D settings is related, in part, to the number of informal contacts people have with others *outside* their own department, discipline, and project team, as well as communication within the team. If the goal is to enhance creativity, then stimulating face-to-face communication among persons whose jobs do not require interaction (a weak organizational bond) is appropriate. In general, those whose jobs require them to interact (strong organizational bond) will do so anyway unless totally blocked by the setting.

Functional diversity was another key organizing principle. Steelcase realized that disciplines such as engineering, marketing, and design tend to attract very different types of people. Each group's work styles, attitudes, and values often are poorly understood (if not ridiculed) by the other groups. Once attitudinal barriers such as these arise, it is very difficult to get groups to communicate and cooperate.

To break down such barriers Steelcase wanted to bring people into closer contact so that they might come to realize that while another group may think and behave differently from them, there is value to the differences and that diversity is needed to generate good ideas and innovative products. So the goal was not "homogenizing" the organization, but helping different groups accept and respect these different ways of thinking and working.

Functional diversity was also intended to support the fact that even within disciplines there can be great differences in personal work style; that is, in how, where, and when people work best. Environmental equity, from this perspective, lies in giving employees access to those physical resources (work spaces and surfaces, privacy, views, storage, display space, and so forth) they need to work effectively, not in giving everyone exactly the same thing.

Another principle guiding the design was that as an individual's work varies over time (day, week, year), the optimal setting for accomplishing that work should vary as well. We don't cook, eat, sleep, and entertain in the same room in our homes. Why should we always discuss a project, type a report, or read a technical article in the same workspace? Steelcase wanted employees to be able to go to the location where, for a specific activity, it made the most sense to work. The underlying

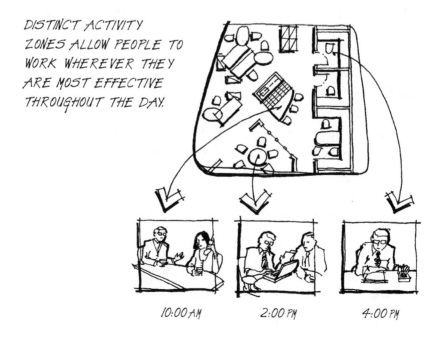

DISTINCT ACTIVITY ZONES ALLOW PEOPLE TO WORK WHEREVER THEY ARE MOST EFFECTIVE THROUGHOUT THE DAY.

10:00 AM   2:00 PM   4:00 PM

premise was that no single office, no matter how well designed, was likely to support equally well all of the tasks and activities and forms of interaction in which workers are involved. Spatial mobility was expected also to increase the likelihood that people would see each other and chat as they moved around the building during the course of their daily activities.

THE CDC PLANNING PROCESS

From the beginning of the CDC project one goal of the project team was to represent key aspects of the rugby model in its own processes and ways of working. This reflects extremely well the organizational ecology principle discussed in Chapter Two: consciously thinking of the process for planning and designing the workplace as a form of organizational development that goes beyond merely collecting information on which to base design decisions. This was reflected in a number of planning process principles, briefly described below.

Decision Hierarchies

The concept of a decision hierarchy is that different classes of decisions should be made at different levels of the organizational hierarchy, but everyone should have some form of decision authority (reflecting a commitment to the concept of empowerment). In the CDC planning process certain fundamental decisions were made by top management, largely without any formal consultation with employees. These included large-scale choices about the site location, the basic building form and materials, and landscaping. It also included main guiding themes such as a commitment to a variety of commons areas, and the decision to use systems furniture in open-plan configuration throughout most of the building. The design and character of commons areas, the policies governing their use, and other interior planning decisions were also ultimately made by management, but with considerable input and review by rank-and-file employees.

Employee involvement took many forms: brief, informal interviews; structured feedback from focus groups to the design team about preliminary designs for work stations and commons areas; completion of survey forms; and review of a full-scale mockup of a section of the building to test employee reactions to a new, specially designed, glare-free glass. Employees provided information about their work styles and task requirements, and they were consulted about the arrangement of furniture components within the work station and commons area. They were not asked for advice about work station size or about the overall building form.

Multiple Work Areas: Private/Project/Shared Space

The concept of employee mobility was encouraged by providing many different work areas for employees to work in, each with a different character and purpose: small individual work stations used in conjunction with a shared commons area, dedicated project rooms, conference rooms, break areas, cafeteria, outside terraces, laboratories, the atrium ("Town Square"), and a resource center ringed by small, fully enclosed offices used on a temporary basis for work requiring high levels of concentration.

Mixed Neighborhoods

The conventional wisdom of adjacency analyses, in which everyone in the same function is located together, was largely abandoned in favor of "mixed neighborhoods" in which people from different disciplines (product engineers, marketers, and designers) shared an area. The intent was not only to foster informal communication across disciplines, but to create working relationships through increased trust and greater tolerance for diversity in work styles and personal styles. Within the neighborhood small clusters of engineers or designers were located together so that cross-disciplinary contact was not bought at the expense of the need professionals have to share information and talk about new developments in their own specialized area.

The Directors' Cluster

Rather than locating all senior management together at the top of the pyramid, in an isolated executive enclave, or locating them with their staff in departmental areas separated from each other, the design team placed a directors' cluster in the middle of the building, easily accessible to others. It was felt that they needed to have easier access to one another (they had previously been in separate buildings) in order to provide coordinated direction to product development efforts. Placing them in the middle was intended to avoid an isolated, "executive row" feeling.

Activity Generators: Town Square/ Cafeteria/Break Areas

The building as a whole was designed to maximize visibility: between floors, to the outside, and into private offices. One set of contributors to maximum visibility are specialized support spaces such as the atrium, cafeteria, and break areas. These are viewed as "activity generators" intended to support serendipitous face-to-face contact. Coffee, white boards, bar-like seating (deliberately not sofas and lounge chairs) are intended to act like magnets that pull people into these areas because they provide necessary and desired resources like coffee and mail.

Corners Commons

Placed in corners of the third floor, the corners commons are multipurpose activity spaces with custom-designed components of movable walls, modular tables, hangable white boards, terminal hookups, and so on. They are intended to serve employees occupying that corner of the floor with furniture they can easily manipulate to create more enclosure or less, a mini-conference room, display and presentation space, or simply a place to relax.

Escalators/Stairs

Elevators and stairs, hidden anonymously behind walls, were replaced with escalators. They were intended to increase the opportunity for establishing visual contact and easy accidental communication with other people and other work areas. They also promote movement between floors, since people tend to use them more readily than they would elevators.

A Different Approach to Adjacencies

Project rooms, conference rooms, laboratories, break areas, and the resource center were distributed throughout the building rather than placing them to minimize travel distance (such as placing a project room immediately adjacent to a laboratory or a particular department or product development group). The intent was to promote functional inconvenience—the idea that movement through a building can be used to encourage personal contact and communication among individuals and groups who, because of weak organizational connections (being in different departments, for example) would not otherwise be likely to have much contact.

As is true with most organizations, there is no way of directly attributing the increased speed of product development that Steelcase has achieved since occupying the new design center to the physical ecology of the center itself. There is no need to. The point of an ecological perspective is that changes in business process and new corporate values and philosophies should be reinforced and supported by the physical ecology of the workplace. So when teamwork, for example, is valued, the physical setting makes it easy for people to actually work together, rather than testing the limits of adaptability and requiring extra energy to overcome environmental roadblocks.

The Limits of Proximity

While some form of increased proximity is an important element of the ecology of collaborative team environments, the problem is knowing what to do when the groups involved are large or, in the case of an aircraft engineering firm we worked with, gigantic. Some preliminary proposals for a new site plan this company commissioned illustrate the limitations of making assumptions about the effects of proximity.

As we discussed the site options with the company's project management group, we learned that the little blocks of space on the plan represented engineering groups of up to five thousand people. We began to realize how easy it is to confuse buildings located adjacent to each other physically with being close to each other functionally in terms of communication and other contacts. Being on the same site is not the same as being under the same roof; nor, if the roof covers several football fields, does being under the same roof contribute much to being "one family."

The point is to think about informal and unplanned communication experientially rather than theoretically. Picture yourself working in one building and just dropping in on someone else in the adjacent building. Imagine getting up, walking down an 800-foot-long corridor, down the stairs, out of the building, along a two-block walkway, into the next building, taking an elevator up two floors, walking down another long corridor, and finally arriving at your destination, only to discover that the person you want to see is out of town. You're not likely to do that very often. Two adjacent buildings hundreds of yards away from each other translate into the kind of proximity that suggests, by looking at a map, that if you live in New York City you are more likely to visit Buffalo than Chicago because Chicago is farther away on the map. Actually, you are not likely to visit either unless you have a good reason, and it is never going to take the form of a spur-of-the-moment tootle up the interstate. But it is easy to forget scale while focusing on plans as abstract relationships.

Informal communication is likely to be stimulated more by facilities decisions centered largely within a manageable-sized facility (and primarily as a function of distance and the strategic placement of some key activity generators such as mailrooms and coffee machines), than by mega-scale site decisions. The two factors most likely to influence unplanned communication are which departments and disciplines are located within a building, and micro-design decisions within the building that have the potential to increase visual contact and communication.

The following are some of the design features that can contribute to effective communication and collaboration.

ACTIVITY MAGNET AREAS

Just as a magnet attracts metal objects within its force field, different kinds of environmental features and amenities can attract people and encourage certain kinds of behavior. Open staircase landings with a view below are good places for serendipitous conversation, chair-height planters encourage us to sit a while. Good design consciously creates these kinds of behavioral force fields.

Communication and Food

Throughout history eating and drinking have been tied in with social contact rituals, and they are no less critical in the workplace. Food and beverages can be strong draws, if located and designed thoughtfully, as Digital Equipment Corporation's small DECSite office outside Stockholm illustrates wonderfully.

Rather than being a dull break room tucked away out of sight—and mind and voice—the break area is in a raised section in the corner of the team room. With its small round tables and café-style chairs, the area indeed feels like a comfortable café—and in the morning it is. Everyone takes turns bringing in the typical Swedish breakfast of cheese and cold cuts, bread and butter, juice, and coffee. Those who want to, arrive between 7:00 A.M. and 8:00 A.M. for a convivial self-serve buffet breakfast. Over food and coffee people chat and joke with each other and gradually ease into the regular working day. Throughout the rest of the day the café is a place for a cup of coffee, an informal meeting, or just an alternative place to read a report or do some other work.

In Digital Equipment's original Finnish "office of the future" an open work area for a sales team had a standup counter and inexpensive patio tables and chairs. Juice and snacks were provided by the company so that employees could take a break whenever they liked in the workspace itself, where they could see others and easily join in and drop out of a conversation without stopping work altogether.

In both these cases the boundary between work and relaxation became much less distinct. People could do "real work" while standing up, drinking coffee and munching on a roll; they could relax by working in a different position (standing, sitting, reclining) or in a different location that increased or reduced contact with other people. The rigid zoning of time and activities that has come to be the norm in most Western offices had been replaced by the idea that food can be eaten at any time of the day (not just lunchtime or when the coffee cart appears) and that eating can enhance work when it occurs not just after work in a restaurant or bar, but in the workplace itself.

Apple Computer's new R&D campus in Cupertino, California, contains a less radical but essentially similar work oasis. High-quality coffees and other beverages are served in the main entrance lobby. This creates an activity zone through which many people pass. Café tables, rather than being invisible in a walled-off cafeteria separate from main circulation paths, are placed in the center of the atrium to enhance visibility and therefore the potential for accidental meetings.

As you walk around the buildings you find other café-style beverage and break areas placed on major circulation routes. In all these cases the normal process of providing snacks has been enhanced by providing high-quality food and beverages in accessible surroundings that are highly pleasant and comfortable, not a tomblike formal break room. As the preliminary data from one of our graduate student's thesis have shown, providing food and beverages, especially when they are high quality, is the simplest and surest way of attracting people to a location.

Shared Services

Just as things to eat and drink exert a strong magnetic force in attracting activity, so do service facilities like mail stations, copy centers, and conference areas that are used on a regular basis by large numbers of employees. These are good activity generators *if their location is chosen carefully*. The key is locating and structuring these services in a way that maximizes the potential for visibility and eye contact among employees.

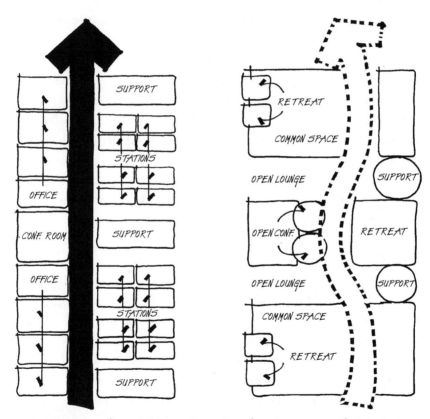

CORRIDORS WITH PERMEABLE BOUNDARIES ALLOW PEOPLE TO SEE WHAT'S GOING ON AS THEY MOVE THROUGH THE BUILDING, CREATE OPPORTUNITIES FOR CONTACT AND COMMUNICATION, AND TRANSFORM A BORING HIGHWAY INTO A LIVELY, STIMULATING JOURNEY.

Europeans have been doing this for a number of years. The Scandinavian Airline Systems (SAS) headquarters near Stockholm has a lively interior "street" that forms the main thoroughfare at ground level through the building. Unlike the soaring atria of many modern corporate buildings, which are impressive as a visual statement but devoid of life and activity because they lead nowhere and provide no reason to linger, SAS's street is lined with shops and cafés—real shops, where you can buy everything from cards to suitcases, and real cafés that serve fresh pastries, fresh-brewed steaming coffee, and hand-cut sandwiches. A bank and travel office are also located here. The feel is less like a staid corporate headquarters and more like the bustling center of a market town.

Digital Equipment Corporation's British headquarters contains a similar kind of internal street, lined with the same kinds of services, but adds small round conference tables up and down the street, where people bring their work for short planned or unplanned meetings. There is good privacy because conversations are masked by the general background noise, but with people passing by on the way to the cafeteria or the bank, you are much more likely to unexpectedly see someone and say, "Call me later." Were these standard corporate services buried throughout the building in various departments, the setting would lack the potential for stimulating not just serendipitous interaction, but also the sense of working in a lively, stimulating environment.

Information Centers as Displayed Thinking

Even when interesting things are going on in corporations, few people may know about them. How can they, if they are invisible? It makes a difference. Hexcel Corporation's honeycomb products are used in everything from fishing poles, baseball bats, and athletic shoes to Boeing aircraft. Shaquille O'Neal's size 22 shoe, with its honeycomb insert in the sole, is a symbol of new product opportunities at a time when these are desperately needed.

Employees like to know where their individual efforts lead, to have a sense of where they fit into the overall scheme of corporate activities. It helps them transcend the feeling of being a tiny cog in a very large and impersonal machine. A simple way to make a company's activities more visible to its members is to concentrate bulletin boards, rotating displays, electronic information monitors, and the like in an accessible central spot that draws people to it and encourages them to talk about what they are seeing and hearing.

The late Walt Disney, realizing that making the activities of the company visible within work groups as well as between groups and for visitors could also directly serve the work process, emphasized the importance of "displayed thinking." Basically, this is the idea that works in progress—in his case storyboards for animation projects—should be displayed where people can look at them whenever and for as long as they want. Disney often did this at night, when everyone had gone home. He would leave notes pinned to the storyboards, raising questions, indicating where he wanted changes, and so on.

Used within the context of a department or building, displayed thinking's potential for generating new ideas and fresh perspectives is enormous. Displayed thinking, especially using the simple anonymous feedback medium of Post-It notes, allows people to challenge ideas and suggest new ones without fear of confrontation. If people want to be contacted, they can encourage that by signing their name.

In today's high-tech world the electronic bulletin board serves the same purpose. With it you can post a question to people with similar interests: "Does anyone know what material might be suitable for a product that needs to be very lightweight and strong, but flexible under extreme temperature variation?" "How many ways are there to get toothpaste back into a tube, and why would we want to?"

With increasing capabilities for multimedia graphics and video, the opportunity to display thinking becomes virtually unlimited. Ideas or images that are visible (such as drawings, graphs, or charts hung on walls) are more likely to influence people's thinking than are occasional formal presentations. They are also more likely to get reactions in process that are useful to the people who are doing the work.

Other general images and visual cues in the work setting can also set a tone either to inhibit or stimulate creativity. If the graphics, pictures, furnishings, and so on all speak to stability and tradition (the founders staring at you from the walls of the boardroom), then it is pretty hard for people to question approaches that are rooted in the past.

It is impossible to program creativity, but it is possible to influence the *pattern* of experiences over time, increasing the probability that new ideas or connections will occur to people who can do something with them that becomes productive. Some of the key features of settings that have been found to encourage creativity are:

- Lots of stimulation: images, ideas, information about what's happening in the world, professional fields, or the marketplace.

- Rich resources to work with so that people don't drop ideas simply for lack of an immediate way to follow through or take the next step.

- A setting that is unconstrained in terms of what it's okay to try or do (few arbitrary rules about what "real work" should look like).

- Controllability in terms of being able to manage distractions or interruptions.

Getting the balance of these features right is difficult, though, because creativity can be influenced by opposite conditions at different stages in a development process. For instance, separation from other parts of the organization can provide focus and promote concentration, or it can isolate people from new ideas and stimulation. To achieve such a balance over time, flexibility is generally an essential feature of the setting. Its design should allow for changes of activities, as well as tightening or loosening boundaries with other parts of the organization. The management process should provide flexibility through policies and social norms that do *not* prescribe one best way to use the workplace, but rather encourage change as conditions dictate.

A Few Rules of Thumb

To summarize this rather wide-ranging discussion, the list of possible elements that can be designed to stimulate teamwork, communication, and collaboration is limited only by our ingenuity. There are, however, a few rules of thumb that are important in creating high-performance workplaces that truly increase the likelihood of communication and teamwork.

Rule #1. Create magnet spots with good stuff in them for drawing people together. If you make a coffee or food center, provide high-quality items.

If you make a seating area, make it comfortable and interesting.

Rule #2. Put magnet spots in the right locations. Usually this means in central locations that are visible and accessible and on the way to other places, not in inconvenient leftover locations that happen to be available and cheap.

Rule #3. Design the contact places well. This may sound obvious, but it is often violated. For instance, don't put displays and information boards in narrow hallways where people who stop to read, watch, and chat will block others trying to use the hallway.

Rule #4. Don't make too many communal spots. For instance, having many beverage areas is handy for individuals, but it reduces the likelihood that people will meet each other while getting something to drink. A few good magnet spots increase the average density of use and therefore the probability of accidental meetings.

Rule #5. Encourage people to use the common facilities. Organizational leaders need to encourage people and set a personal example by using magnet spots, informal areas, and other commons areas so that employees won't feel that they will pay a price for talking to others during work hours. Help them feel that this *is* a part of the job.

The Issue of Organizational Culture

Of course, these rules of thumb make no sense unless you start from the assumption that it is a good thing for people to communicate informally and that this is not inefficient behavior to be driven out of the system. Creating settings that increase the probability of unplanned contacts requires not only providing good places for chatting informally, but making it legitimate to do so. The legitimacy issue is not minor. Creating a truly lively, active center to an organization's spaces requires a delicate balance between physical design and social/cultural factors that influence how the design is actually used.

We work with a client that has two informal, rather pleasant sitting areas in their space, at opposite ends of the building. One gets used all the time and serves as the focal gathering point for many groupings that cut across departmental lines. It is the place where a lot of informal coordination happens. The other area is almost never used—in fact, we have never seen anyone except ourselves actually sitting on the couch or chairs. It is located fairly near to the offices of the chairman and the president, and it was also furnished with less comfortable pieces than the active area. We say "was" because some changes were made, including more comfortable chairs and a different arrangement. So far, however, it has made no difference. We suspect it is because the norms of the group dictate that you should not look like you are socializing where the top executives can see you. This is ironic, since the chairman and president tell us that they want to see the barriers between groups reduced and would love to see more informal contact as a good means to that end. They like the fact that people get together and wish they could stimulate more of it at their end of the floor.

The point is simple. Physical design, by itself, will not change behavior patterns and guarantee teamwork. It can make some activities more likely than others, and when it is in tune with the social system, it can create the kind of lively, interactive setting that supports teamwork and collaboration.

CHAPTER SIX

Creating a Healthy Environment

We have been discussing various facets of the workplace as a tool for accomplishing tasks and fulfilling the organization's mission while using resources wisely. If this thinking becomes loaded too much toward a mechanistic or engineering framework, there is a danger of forgetting an important point: organizations are made up of collections of human beings.

There is a wealth of evidence to suggest that people are not like drill presses or computers, where under the right conditions you can turn them on in the morning and let them run at the same speed all day. People have physiological and psychological rhythms to their days. These rhythms vary with individuals and within the same person on different days of the week or at different times of the year, so that they are not programmable.

Therefore, another major function of the work setting is to provide good health and high-quality experiences for its people. It is hard to be a successful, high-quality organization if you are wearing down your members in the process.

It should therefore be both a practical and an ethical concern of organizational leaders that the work setting promote the well-being of its users: physiological health and safety, mental health, the ability to grow and develop, and high-quality work experiences as the normal pattern of work life rather than the exception.

Of course employee well-being is influenced by several other major factors besides organizational ecology, including managerial style, the demands of the work, individual preferences, organizational culture and policies, and so on. But for our purposes here, we are emphasizing the need for leaders to be aware of the impact of the total work setting (physical and social) on people's health and sense of well-being.

In the history of business in the United States there has been varied awareness of the impact of work settings on employee health. Until recently, the majority of concerns focussed on highly hazardous or noxious working conditions, such as coal mining, producing chemicals, rigging the steel on tall buildings, and the like. Even in these areas, there were periods when the risks were simply treated as part of the territory. If you chose to do that sort of work, then you were taking on all the associated risks. Only gradually has it become accepted that many occupational risks can and should be controlled, shaping how the work is done and how resources are allocated toward making the setting safe for the workers who use it.

Along with this point of view, there has been a shift in relative priorities, so that personal safety now commands more resources than were previously thought to be efficient or necessary. This shift has also been institutionalized and enforced through national legislation such as the Occupational Safety and Health Act (OSHA) and the universal access provisions of the Americans with Disabilities Act (ADA), both of which set standards that employers must meet or face being fined.

This concern with worker safety and health has been expanded in recent years to include less obvious settings: the general office-type environments in which the majority of today's workers spend their time. In the arena of basic workplace conditions, there have been a number of particular concerns, including:

- Air quality (air flow, rate of exchange, purity, and so on).

- Temperature in the workplace (comfort, appropriateness for the task, and so on).

- Ambient sound conditions (noise levels, ability to hear necessary information, and so on).

- Lighting conditions (access to natural light, visibility of work, controlling glare on video screens, and so on).

- Physical body positions in repetitive work (posture while seated, location of materials and shelves, computers and keyboards, and so on).

It is now generally recognized that if any of these factors is not well designed and people spend a good bit of time each day in that particular setting, the cumulative impact on their health can be substantial. An example is carpal tunnel syndrome, an extremely painful condition of the wrist that comes from long periods of entering or manipulating data at computer terminals. It is not as obvious as miners' black lung disease, but it can affect almost all of a person's daily activities. Providing ergonomic keyboards and wrist supports is one way to address such problems, as is the redesign of the job itself to minimize the need for employees to do repetitive tasks hours on end. In Sweden, providing a healthy, supportive, ergonomic environment has taken yet a different turn.

The Natural Office

There is no research anywhere in the world that shows that people are more productive when they are sitting in a bolt upright position. There is, in fact, human-factors research that indicates that a reclining position helps reduce pressure and strain on the back, as does standing. Yet most of our offices are designed as though sitting with a straight back is, if not the only, certainly the primary position for working effectively. Sitting upright at a desk undoubtedly has its place. But a cursory look around home offices—where work can be organized more to reflect people's own work styles—is likely to find people sprawled on a sofa or leaning back in their chair, feet up, listening to music, with something to drink and nibble on nearby.

The fundamental fact is that there is no single best way to work effectively. Yet enormous effort, energy, money, time, and emotion are spent in designing furniture and offices all over the world that deny this simple fact.

Our belief about the *appearance* of working hard is deep-rooted. It really is moral in nature. It springs from religious concepts concerning the virtue of hard work and being an upstanding (that is to say, righteous) person. The word "work" in most countries is the antonym for "play." The goal has been to encourage efficiency and to eliminate all wasted effort; that is, everything that does not appear to directly contribute to an end product.

Socializing among workers, within this moral and management context, became synonymous with wasted effort. People were paid to work, not to talk. Certainly, people were not paid to be comfortable. That was what you did *after* finishing work. Then you could relax, put your feet up, read the newspaper, have a drink, and talk with friends and family. Well, all that is beginning to change.

For example, DECSite, a new spinoff company within Digital Equipment Corporation Sweden, has recently created a work environment that departs from the typical approach to ergonomics. Rather than good ergonomics being defined as supporting someone in a standard sitting position, at DECSite Sweden it has been defined as supporting people comfortably in whatever position they choose to work. Strange-looking "pipe" chairs (they look like giant pipe cleaners that have been twisted into a chairlike form) allow people to sit with their legs thrown over an arm of the chair, their arms over the back, or sideways on the chair. There is no assumption that all employees should sit facing each other with their backs more or less straight. The same is true of the ergonomic desk chairs provided. These are designed to allow people to sit sideways on the chair, or to sit comfortably with the back of the chair in front, with their arms resting on the back.

Computers are located in the ceiling, and are let down to whatever height people prefer at any particular point, including when they are standing. Drinking coffee is not considered a break from work, requiring a trip to a break room or cafeteria. Instead, there is a raised platform in a corner of the open office area furnished with typical café tables and chairs. Staff sit here to drink coffee and chat, to read, or to simply work in a different place for a time.

The whole environment is incredibly efficient, in terms of space use, but it is also designed from the ground up to support a natural way of working, one in which each individual chooses, for a given task and point in time, how and where he or she wishes to work. There is no assumption that sitting in a lounge chair with your feet up is a poor way to conduct a telephone conversation, read a book, or just think about a problem. Conversely, there is no assumption that you *should* work in these positions, either. Each person decides for him or herself.

In this kind of work environment managers must focus on real productivity: what actually gets done as opposed to how people look doing it.

Creating a "natural" office takes courage, because it flouts convention, including the practice of promoting image for image's sake. It may also be difficult to find interior designers and architects who are able to break out of the boundaries of their own training and experience. In several truly innovative natural offices we have studied, the clients had to fire some perfectly competent architects because they were unable to propose plans that violated their sense of aesthetic order and what constituted a professional work environment.

The natural office shifts the focus from a fairly narrow definition of what is considered a professional way to work to embrace a principle that says people are different and work effectively in different ways. It is like the difference in our own homes between the formality of the front parlor, where we put on our public face, and the informality of the family room or the den, the place we gravitate to because it is friendly, comfortable, and genuinely supports what we are doing.

Sick-Building Syndrome

"Sick-building syndrome" refers to buildings with a level of toxic substances in the air that induces a number of symptoms in those who are susceptible: allergies, shortness of breath, headaches, dizziness, undue fatigue, and the like. Instead of treating these as individual, unrelated occurrences of illness, facilities managers are now seeking causes of such patterns in the ambient work environment and then striving to correct the setting.

Organizations and governments in Europe have tended to be ahead of the United States in terms of developing enforceable legal standards for the impact of work settings on employees. For example, research has shown that people deprived of natural sunlight for long periods tend to become depressed and less able to function. In a number of European countries it has therefore been mandated by law that employees must be able to see natural daylight from their personal work location. This is several jumps ahead of where things stand in the United States today.

Personal Comfort and Personal Control

American companies are beginning to make the healthy setting a visible theme in their relationship or contract with their workforce. For example, the West Bend Insurance Company in West Bend, Wisconsin, has recently created a new home office using the theme of employees' well-being in the workplace as a major focus for the project.

The company created a high-quality overall setting with good exterior views and pleasant interior views and finishes. But what is most interesting is the approach to providing good immediate surroundings for workers. Instead of trying to create perfect conditions for everyone with some average settings, West Bend installed work stations that allow occupants to control not only work surface heights and chair settings, but also individual temperature, air flow, task lighting, and ambient noise level in their work areas through use of a Johnson Controls system called the Personal Environment Module (or PEM). West Bend leaders based this effort on the assumption that real comfort cannot be provided through average settings, but only through individual control of one's immediate surroundings.

Before-and-after studies have shown consistent productivity gains from the new environment. They have also found strong sentiments and expectations in employees: once they had the PEMs, people did not want to go back to their old, low-influence mode, even as part of a temporary on–off experiment. Those assigned to the "off" group threatened to stay home until their PEMs were reconnected.

Another approach that enhances personal control is loosening constraints on how people can use their workplaces, such as doing away with prescribed break times during the day and letting people get a change of pace when they need it rather than when top management has prescribed that they ought to need it. One company did away with the mobile "break cart" that used to bring around beverages and snacks, and found that employees were more willing to take seriously company pronouncements about "empowerment." The cart had been a low-level irritant for years, representing an inconsistent symbol of management's need to control behavior while saying they were trying to loosen up.

Encouraging people to influence their own immediate environments and their "time-in/time-out" patterns for using them is an important element of a more healthy workplace. It is particularly helpful in roles where the tasks are inherently high-paced or high-stress, such as commodities trading or coping with disgruntled customers. The people who know most about when a change of scene or break is needed are those involved in the action. It is important both to provide spots to get out of the line of fire and to make it legitimate for someone to do so without being treated as a slacker or goof-off.

There was a period some years ago when think tanks and quiet rooms were a novelty fad, but they often went unused because the organization's norms about looking busy did not change. The underlying concept of providing a variety of spots so that people can change their pace or work pattern during the day is becoming accepted without a lot of fanfare. It is a way both to stay healthy and to be more productive by being more alive and awake when it's "time in."

Safety and Security

There is also increasing concern about providing employees with a secure setting where they are not subject to attacks on either property or person. The perceived rise in violent crime has been one force in the moving of some corporate headquarters from center-city locations to the suburbs. Security systems have been beefed up to control unauthorized access to corporate facilities, even at the cost of employees themselves feeling more regimented and excluded from free movement within their own system.

Employees often feel most at risk not when they are in the workplace, but in the process of arriving and leaving. Those who go home after dark feel especially vulnerable. This is a real issue for companies such as software design firms where many members do not work to a traditional 9-to-5 pattern (or any pattern at all). Solutions include better lighting for parking lots, secured parking areas with guards or electronic surveillance, and so on. We know one company that was able to exchange one of its parking lots located several blocks away from their building with a parking lot nearby that was owned by the city. This trade cut down the distance and improved the route employees traveled from their cars to the office. Employee shuttles and accompanying security guards are also used in high-risk situations.

The point is that people's experiences with their work environment include the process of getting there and leaving as well as time spent on the premises. Even if they are not personally attacked, they can suffer stress from worrying about being vulnerable to such attacks. It behooves a company's leadership to treat such fears as a factor in designing and managing support facilities. For example, creating passageways and stairwells with glass walls helps people feel less isolated, better able to see whether anyone is lurking, and less likely to be attacked with no one able to see what is happening to them.

Physical Fitness

People's lifestyles are obviously a factor in whether they remain healthy. Organizational leaders have been shifting their stance in this area away from assuming that it is a personal problem to stay fit and should be done outside working hours, toward the sense that it is a joint problem owned by both the person and the organization. Demanding schedules can work against people fitting in exercise times outside the workplace. Another way to encourage fitness is therefore to provide facilities and promote policies that encourage their use by as many members as possible within the context of the workplace.

This effort may be as simple as providing changing and shower facilities so that people can choose when to run or walk for exercise and still go back to work (versus only doing it from home or a health club). If there is an outside health club nearby, some companies provide memberships rather than installing their own facilities. Others have gone the full route of installing both changing and exercise facilities and staffing them with professionals in health, nutrition, and exercise physiology.

All of these efforts are based on the recognition that the pattern of people's total daily experiences affects their health and sense of well-being. If the organization's leaders expect members to spend a high percentage of their waking hours in their work roles, it makes good sense long term to provide settings that make daily patterns more healthy. Healthy workers are likely to be more productive while at work, and less likely to miss work or require medical care. This also helps in reducing insurance claims and premiums.

One easy test of whether there is a serious commitment to this approach is how and where exercise facilities are set up. In the past they were often treated as an afterthought, placed in leftover space such as an otherwise unused basement. Happily, this appears to be changing. For example, we work with a research and development firm that placed very good exercise equipment in a space with large windows looking out on a beautiful scene with a pond, rolling lawns, and occasional ornamental geese. It also has convenient access to outdoors for runners and is near the central entrance so that it is easy to find.

All of these details have the same intent: making the setup as inviting and convenient as possible so that people will use it regularly. Health benefits don't come from exercising when you have nothing better to do, but rather from establishing a pattern of regular activity that serves as a recharger of energy as well as a maintainer of fitness. The health of members should just naturally be considered to be a component of organizational health.

Natural Light

When we consider the cumulative effects of working in a setting day after day, a person's exposure to natural light and views becomes a major factor. We have already referred to studies showing that humans function better when exposed to natural light. Beyond this there is also the positive effect on the spirit of being able to see the outside: a sense of connection, a feeling for one's surroundings, being in touch with the weather and the flow of the day, and the like. We have already argued the case for gaining flexibility by uncoupling windows from the system's status language. This also helps to provide a higher-quality level of light to the total population, not just to a select few.

A similar approach applied to the windows issue has already been taken at governmental levels in northern Europe. In several countries there are laws requiring that all employees must have access to natural daylight at their personal workplaces. This stems from a widespread social concern for a healthy work environment that promotes a sense of well-being (not just one that does not cause specific illnesses).

In the United States, the laws are typically not so clear on this issue, but some companies are coming to a similar conclusion about the importance of natural light. One new policy approach has been to allocate windows to those workers who, because of the nature of their tasks, tend to spend the day rooted in their workplaces. In practice this often means accountants, secretaries, and other support staff. This provides the biggest benefit to those for whom it makes the most difference, which can be a nice antidote to a demanding, stressful job situation.

In order to allow natural light to reach the interior spaces away from the external walls, some companies have adopted an interesting design principle: closed offices will not be built on window walls, but only off the interior core, often with glass fronts so occupants still get natural light. The areas adjacent to the window walls are used for open-plan layouts and walkways so the light is not blocked. Others have taken a partial step in this direction by requiring that closed offices, if built on the periphery, must have a glass inside wall, so that natural light still gets to others working in the interior areas.

In situations where access to external daylight is not feasible, such as in central-core areas of large floors, there is also increased care in the design of lighting. One trend is the installation of light sources that produce light at roughly 5600 degrees Kelvin, the same temperature as sunlight.

Easing Life's Logistical Stresses

Another aspect of today's organizational settings that is aimed at enhancing employee well-being is the expansion of services and facilities to help people deal with the small but stressful errands that have become tricky problems in today's world of two-career families. Companies are helping members cope with the logistics of life in order to reduce the level of distraction and stress involved.

For example, we have recently seen several companies that contracted for dry cleaning and laundry services, with pickup and delivery to the office. This seems like an odd area for a company to get into, but it turns out to be a convenience that employees like a lot. It appears to solve a host of timing problems so that people can focus on what they are doing at work and at home. Similarly, travel services are being provided for family and other personal trips in addition to the more typical work-related travel arrangements.

While these efforts are, strictly speaking, not related to the physical design of the workplace, they do influence the total setting—physical and social—that makes up the environment for people's work lives. The importance of such services is also affected by the workplace's location. Employees in a remote suburban or rural location face greater day-to-day logistics problems than those who work in a center-city location with a dense array of services nearby.

In a similar vein, other companies are experimenting with a "concierge" role: a person who will attempt to solve employees' logistical problems, such as getting theater or sports tickets, dropping and picking up a car for servicing, meeting repair people at the home to let them do their work, or whatever. This appears to be the kind of environmental amenity that people really appreciate, since the service is defined by the users' needs, not by what management thinks the people will want.

For those employees who are parents, the most important area for logistical support is of course day care for young children. This has become a major issue for many families because of the increasing incidence of both parents having jobs. Company leaders who initially shied away from day care as too expensive or complicated are coming to consider it as worth the effort because of its contribution to the well-being and effectiveness of the workforce. As one executive told us, it is an important element in being the "employer of choice" in their region.

When it comes to day-care services, there are a number of specific design considerations: whether to run it yourself, on site versus off site, how visible to make it if it is on site, ease of access for leaving and collecting children, and so on. If you are going to bother to do it, take care to do it well. New service companies such as Boston's Work/Family Directions have been created to help individuals, corporations, and communities provide high-quality services and facilities related to work and family issues.

These various logistical supports can tend to sound like the old-time paternalism of the "company town," and some may indeed feel that way to employees. But by and large today's efforts seem to have less of the underlying control message, "We know what you should want, and we'll give it to you when we think you should need it." To be effective, these modern programs try to emphasize personal choice and support rather than top-down direction and control. The point is to reduce the amount of stress that employees experience in balancing work and home demands, not to create more problems with unrealistic expectations.

High-Quality Design

Employee well-being and high-quality work experiences are shaped by the workplace beyond each person's own desk or office. In more than a few organizations the cafeteria is considered the lunch option of last resort, not because of the low quality of the food, but because the layout and decoration are so dreary. People use terms such as "the cave," "the pit," or "the hole" when discussing whether or not to eat in these kinds of places. Typically these areas are dark, dingy, and cramped; you could never confuse them with an uplifting place to spend time. Organizations that tolerate such places seem to view food and beverages as fuel: fill up the tank and roar away.

In other organizations cafeterias and break areas are truly relaxing, cheery places. The Japanese term for informal break areas—they call them "refresh" areas—more closely captures what should be the underlying intent of these kinds of spaces. Well-designed cafeterias and break areas have the potential to energize and relieve tension. They can also be used all day long as a pleasant, informal meeting spot, one that many organizations could not afford to provide on a stand-alone basis. We are not talking about grasping for luxury here, but simply about creating places that are light, cheery, interesting, and pleasant to use.

In general, high-quality, refreshing environments are ones that:

- Pay attention to details. Typically the fire stair is unfinished but might be used were it more pleasant. In some Japanese buildings these stairs are fitted out with murals or with fun, quirky games like a target to try to jump up and touch.

- Are well lit. Natural light is nearly always best, unless the point is to create a quiet, reflective mood with softer lighting. Again, we have visited a Japanese satellite office equipped with a meditation room where the users can control not only the light level but totally different moods by changing the color of the light source.

- Are human scale. Very large and undefined spaces tend to overwhelm. A large cafeteria, for example, can be subdivided into smaller areas with their own distinctive character.

- Have interesting things to look at, such as changing displays. Best of all, "interesting" is defined by the actual users.

- Contain features that allow people to make their own choices about how to use them. For example, a well-designed "scramble" mode cafeteria, or some free-standing modular furniture that the employees can rearrange themselves.

Many other principles could be enumerated, some general and some specific to certain activities or populations. It is useful for leaders to make a list of such principles that they feel are important for their enterprise, and then rate their work settings on how well they match the principles. This can form the basis for upgrading the setting, without necessarily requiring a large capital expense.

A Note About Green Buildings

There is an increasing emphasis in both Europe and North America on creating so-called green buildings—work settings that do not pollute or degrade resources in the environment. These efforts include:

- Using building materials that do not deplete fragile resources such as the rain forests.

- Instituting recycling programs that keep unused trash to a minimum.

- Using high-efficiency energy systems and renewable sources such as sunlight.

- Using safe, nontoxic chemicals in industrial processing.

- Using natural materials in indoor furniture, so they can be reused in other forms.

Companies have also put new emphasis on designing and situating workplaces that fit especially well into their surroundings, disturbing as little of the natural system as possible. Two of the best examples we have seen are located in the upper Midwest: Steelcase in western Michigan and West Bend Insurance in Wisconsin. Each has been designed to keep the prairie grasses and wildflower meadows around its structures. The effect is extremely pleasant and soothing for both occupants and visitors. They also are maintaining examples of a vanishing natural resource.

In Closing

Almost any element in the workplace, physical or social, can affect employee well-being: design, management processes, culture, policies, patterns of tasks, peak load demands, and so on. From a workplace perspective, the key for leaders is to seek feedback from users, have models of healthy environments in mind, and take the trouble to treat this issue seriously on a regular basis.

Being committed to a healthy setting is ultimately nothing more than simply good business. It is worthwhile from a productivity and efficiency standpoint because people can focus better and bring more productive energy to the job role. We also believe that in the long run it is important in a philosophical sense that the organization's fundamental identity should be that of a system that enhances rather than degrades the health of its members. This truly helps make the organization an entity worth maintaining and encourages people to commit their best efforts to its mission.

CHAPTER SEVEN

Supporting Remote Work

Bell Atlantic, AT&T, Travelers Insurance, IBM, Steelcase, Ernst and Young, Andersen Consulting, and many other companies are fundamentally rethinking the way their workplaces are planned, designed, and managed. While the transformation in the amount and type of space and real estate these companies are using is the visible tip of the iceberg, the real mountain that lies just beneath the surface is made up of new assumptions about how best to convene work in time and space.

Telecommuting programs, neighborhood work centers, and the virtual office are partly a solution to real estate problems, partly a sales pitch for new technology, and partly a means of improving air quality and traffic congestion. But they also represent a transformation of the nature of work itself. These new ways of working are being driven by unprecedented competitive pressures generating the need to dramatically reduce costs while improving the quality and level of products and services provided—all with fewer workers, representing a wider range of backgrounds and expectations, being asked to do more. Take Novex,* for example.

---

*Novex is a composite of several real companies. This example was used, in part, in an earlier report by M. Joroff, M. Louargand, S. Lambert, and F. Becker, Strategic Management of the Fifth Resource: Corporate Real Estate. *Atlanta, Ga.: Industrial Development Research Council, 1993.*

Novex

Novex products are known to just about everyone. A highly respected and very successful manufacturing company, Novex has had a sterling reputation for product innovation and customer support. Its generous employee benefits packages, above-average salaries, and general policy of promoting from within have helped it attract and retain some of the best and brightest technical and managerial people in the country.

While its products have been innovative, its approach to planning, designing, and managing its workplace has been conventional. With the exception of the development laboratories and the state-of-the-art manufacturing facilities, both of which have always housed the latest and most sophisticated equipment and are recognized by everyone in the firm as an invaluable tool for enabling Novex to prosper, its office facilities have been viewed essentially as an uninteresting but necessary form of corporate overhead.

This does not mean the office facilities were inexpensive. The company's commitment to excellence in manufacturing and new-product development has been reflected in a companywide mindset that values the concept of quality. Quality can take many forms in Novex, but in general these have been on the expensive side: the longest-lasting carpet, highly visible and central locations, and expensive finishes and materials in public areas.

Considerations of rank and status are embedded in the amount and quality of space allocated. The higher one rises in the organization, the larger the office, the greater the degree of enclosure, the more expensive the furnishings, the better the view. Using workplace design to communicate status distinctions has been justified functionally: managers argue that customers want to see and meet the management in large, well-appointed, beautiful offices. Also, allocating space by rank is believed to act as an incentive for younger staff, giving them something to aspire to, and differences in office size are considered necessary to provide the necessary confidentiality in sensitive meetings.

Over the years flexibility and adaptability to changing organizational requirements have been met by short leases in nonowned buildings. Up until a few years ago Novex maintained its own highly qualified staff of carpenters, painters, electricians, and plumbers and their shops so that work could be quickly and easily scheduled. Systems furniture was purchased so that offices could be quickly reconfigured over a weekend to accommodate a departmental reorganization or the addition or elimination of staff. The existing space standards inevitably entitled at least some of the staff to move to an office of a different size with different kinds of furniture.

These policies and practices, which had worked well for Novex for many years, started to unravel about five years ago, as did many of their other entrenched organizational practices. One result of the recession in the late 1980s was that cost reduction became the corporate mantra. Total quality management programs involving reengineering of the product development and manufacturing processes were initiated to reduce costs and speed the introduction of new products.

One of the most visible signs of these efforts was headcount reduction throughout the organization. Along with this came a new interest by senior management in learning more precisely how much the workplace, viewed as a potentially rich source for reducing corporate overhead expenses, actually cost.

As the figures began to appear, they surprised Novex's executive management. Facility costs had risen much more quickly than revenue. In response, a new position was recently created for a kind of real estate czar. With strong support from the highest levels of management, her mission is to rethink from the ground up Novex's approach to planning, designing, and managing its real estate portfolio. She is now working to resolve a number of dilemmas embedded in Novex's workplace practices.

Dilemmas in Developing and Implementing New Workplace Strategies

The story of Novex is the story of untold numbers of American organizations. It captures the range of hard decisions facing not just real estate and facility professionals today, but also organizational leaders at the highest levels. We choose to use the word "dilemma" to characterize the workplace choices organizations must make because, as the dictionary suggests, it reflects so well the current problem; namely, being faced with "a difficult or doubtful choice; a state of things in which evils or obstacles present themselves on every side, and it is difficult to determine what course to pursue" (Whitehall, 1951, p. 485). This is the situation most organizations face today: hard choices without clear answers, and yet no choice but to choose.

The choices Novex is facing include understanding how best to:

- Reduce costs

- Maintain environmental quality

- Accommodate unpredictable organizational change

- Manage control, especially between corporate and field sites

- Improve building performance and employee performance

- Accommodate a workforce much more diverse in age, gender, ethnicity, and lifestyle

- Exploit new information technologies that have the potential to support more flexible and remote work patterns

It takes a fundamental paradigm shift to identify and implement workplace strategies that alleviate the pressures organizations are facing as they struggle to become more competitive. In this shift the workplace becomes a dynamic tool for supporting and even stimulating new ways of working, rather than a fixed asset whose performance is assessed primarily in terms of how much money it costs or generates.

The changes associated with such a paradigm shift are immense. The linear world most of us have found so comforting is vanishing. Our most fundamental beliefs about the way work is structured, including where and when it is done, are in the process of becoming irrelevant. Organizational leaders can choose to view this intricate web of pressures as suffocating, and ignore or fight them. Or they can choose to see them as liberating, and embrace and exploit them as they explore new working practices such as home-based telework, telework centers, and virtual offices. The common thread linking these new time/space work patterns is that they all involve some form of remote work.

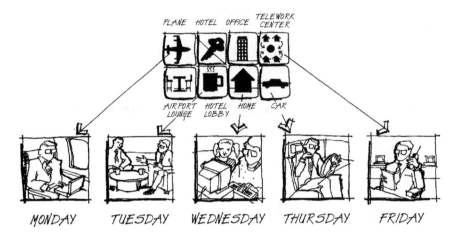

INTEGRATED WORKPLACE STRATEGIES PROVIDE AN ARRAY OF WORKPLACE OPTIONS FOR THOSE WORKING REMOTELY.

Home-Based Telework

Ten years ago, when the onslaught of personal computers was just beginning, home-based telecommuting was heralded as a kind of organizational panacea to support more women working at home, especially those with young children. Today telework is finally beginning to be implemented on a large scale.

Recently, for example, Bell Atlantic offered telecommuting to 16,000 of its employees. Edward Weiner, a senior policy analyst with the U.S. Department of Transportation, cites federal government studies indicating that the number of American workers telecommuting is estimated to increase from 2 million in 1992 to somewhere between 7 and 10 million in 2002, an increase from about 1.5 percent of the workforce to 10.5 percent (Weiner, 1993). A 1991 teleworking study from LINK Resources in New York estimated the number of teleworkers in the United States at close to 6 million people in 1991, almost 5 percent of the total U.S. workforce, with an average annual growth rate of 29 percent. In 1993 this figure increased, reaching 7.9 million teleworkers. Most of these increases are coming from large organizations (over 1,000 employees) and very small organizations (fewer than 10 employees). About 22 percent of Fortune 500 companies have formal teleworking programs (Miller, 1992).

Telecommuting responds to a number of organizational pressures in addition to workforce demographics. It reduces long commutes and the lost time, air quality, traffic congestion, and personal stress associated with them. It can help attract workers ranging from the disabled to the single parent or suburbanite who might not otherwise be willing or able to participate in the workforce.

GTE Telephone Operations in Irving, Texas, has put together a summary of its research on what the typical teleworker looks like (Romei, 1992):

- Very likely married, and within the baby-boomer age range of thirty-five to forty-five

- Well-educated

- Predominantly white-collar professionals

- Equally likely to be male or female

There are lots of myths surrounding teleworking, particularly concerning why people do it and how it affects their performance. The increasing number of studies that have been done paint a picture that challenges many of these myths. The regional Bell operating companies such as Mountain Bell and Pacific Bell report an average increase of about 30 percent in the amount of work done by telecommuters, as well as a reduction in nonproductive time resulting from office distractions and absenteeism.

A study by Joanne H. Pratt Associates (Pratt, 1993) found that:

- Teleworkers do not work at home as an alternative to child care. The majority of teleworkers with small children place them outside the home, either in a relative's home or in day-care centers, on the days that they work at home.

- Teleworkers do not slack off on work at home; on average, teleworkers work about the same amount of time as nonteleworkers.

- Teleworking does not decrease participants' chances for promotion. Almost 40 percent of male teleworkers were promoted in 1988 compared to 27 percent of nonteleworking males. This pattern was also true of women: 34 percent of female teleworkers received promotions compared to 21 percent of female nonteleworkers.

In part, this trend can be explained by the fact that the majority of teleworkers hold management jobs and were initially allowed to work from home because they had demonstrated their initiative and high performance. An evaluation of the federal government's flexiwork project found, however, that performance ratings increased among employees whose in-office performance had previously only been rated as average.

Organizations vary in the types of equipment and furniture they provide to their employees. Some companies provide a fully equipped home office; others will require the employees to furnish and equip their home office themselves. The kind of office furnishings and equipment provided include:

- Furniture (ergonomic seating, desks, lighting, storage)

- Equipment (computer, printer, modem, fax, telephone, answering machine)

- Rent and utility supplement (in the Netherlands government pilot program)

- Additional telephone lines

Done on a large scale, telecommuting can significantly reduce an organization's facility costs. This is true even when companies provide their telecommuting employees with furniture and equipment for the home. AT&T estimates that the average *one-time* expense of this equipment (computers, telephone lines, modem)—about $6,000—is offset by the *annual* cost savings in office space—also about $6,000. Thus, there is a one-year payback to telecommuting, after which time the company is presumably saving at least several thousand dollars per employee per year. Even if the company provides the telecommuter with furniture for the home office, the payback is still somewhere between one and two years.

HOME-BASED TELEWORK NOT FOR EVERYONE

Given these benefits, telework would seem the perfect occupancy strategy. Unfortunately, by itself it is not. Some people do not have the space at home; some want to separate their work from their family life. Others find the allure of the refrigerator, the television, or the lawnmower too strong. Working at home can be socially isolating, and where the work is part of a team or group activity, full-time remote work may undermine team effectiveness.

Organizations are also concerned about liability issues related to the difficulty of ensuring compliance with safety and ergonomic standards or regulations, as well as about protecting the security and confidentiality of information. And finally, many managers are puzzled about remote supervision and the effect of telecommuting on group dynamics, teamwork, and corporate identity. The idea that if the employee cannot be seen she must not be working is deeply ingrained in many managers' minds, despite the fact that were this same test applied to the managers themselves, who are out of the office 50 percent or more of the time, they would have to be considered among the least productive of all workers!

For all these reasons, telecommuting in the form of full-time home-based work is unlikely to be a viable solution by itself. In fact, the vast majority of American corporate telecommuters work at home only an average of one to two days a week. The popular negative stereotype of telework—someone working alone at home five days a week, glued to a computer monitor, isolated from friends and co-workers—is a myth. An interesting question, one largely unasked by telecommuting advocates, is where are the telecommuters the other three to four days a week, and how is the design and organization of these workplaces supporting effective work processes?

TIME/ACTIVITY PATTERNS

Most home-based telecommuters return to their base office periodically to talk with their managers and co-workers, to share information, and to catch up on office news and gossip. They also work out of their car, and in hotels and airports, as well as on their customers' premises, as they meet with clients and customers and their own staff and managers. In effect, their work cuts across conventional space-time images of the workplace. Most telework programs do not. They tend to focus on *not* working at the office, without understanding how using remote settings, like the home, may affect the use patterns and design of settings like the central office, which are now only used periodically.

For example, it makes little sense for people who have been working at home, independently, to come into the office and do exactly the same kind of work there they were doing at home. For teleworkers the days in the office are likely to be more productive if they are viewed as a time for communication and interaction, to share insights gleaned from customers and client interaction, to review work done at home, to clarify goals and targets, and plan next steps. If these kinds of interactive activities are important, then the office may more sensibly be designed as a club than as a place for individual work.

This would mean turning our concept of the conventional office inside out. Rather than devoting the bulk of the office space to individual work stations and offices, with a small percentage of space allocated for formal and informal meeting areas, the primary function of the central office space might become support of communication and interaction. In this kind of an office, areas for individual, more concentrative work would become the "support" space for the more team-oriented interactive spaces.

This is exactly what has happened with our own work space at Cornell. About two years ago the staff and director of the International Workplace Studies Program traded in their own individual offices, including one of the largest corner offices in the department, for a single open team room fitted out with several computer work stations, mobile telephones, a large conference table, and an informal area to relax. The success of this lively, interactive team room cannot be understood without understanding that it exists in conjunction with the opportunity to work at home, with equipment provided by the research program, including high-speed modems that connect the computers at home to the university's networks and to Internet. Once there, one can literally be anywhere in the world.

It is the ability to do highly concentrative work at home, supported by proper technology and supportive management practices, that makes the highly interactive nature of this team office so successful. And those who do not or cannot work at home can use another small, unassigned office in the department for their concentrative work. It is equipped only with a small table, a telephone, and a laptop computer.

If we consider all the places people work, they are part of what might be called a system of "loosely coupled settings." These settings—the

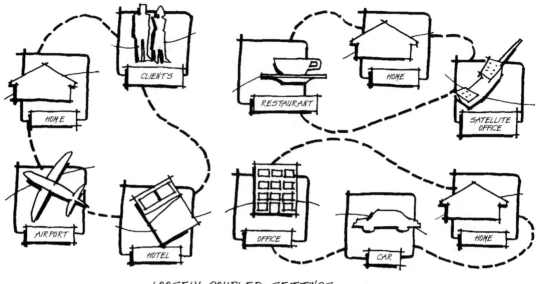

LOOSELY COUPLED SETTINGS

home, the neighborhood work center, the car or airplane, and the central office—are linked physically by the movement of employees who work in these settings over the course of a day, a week, or the life of a project; and by the electronic movement of information through e-mail, voice mail, videoconferencing, telephone, and fax.

LOOSELY COUPLED SETTINGS

For telecommuting or any other new workplace pattern to serve the organization well, it must become part of an integrated workplace strategy that senior management views as helping the organization achieve its fundamental business objectives, *in addition to* improving regional air quality, employees' quality of life, and even individual productivity. This requires a policy of allowing people to work at home, fostering new management practices, providing the associated training to make them possible, and instituting the right kind of information technologies. In Chapter Nine we will examine the importance of making a commitment to exploit time and space in other settings, such as telework and neighborhood work centers, that are consciously and deliberately managed as a single, integrated workplace strategy.

Telework Centers

Telework centers take many forms.* The common characteristic is that rather than working at home, in a central or branch office, or in a temporary office like a hotel, car, or restaurant, employees are provided with access to a professional work environment close to where they live. Some may work at these sites full time; others may split their time among the telework center, the home, a central headquarters, and a client's office. The telework centers can also be a drop-in office, used when needed on an irregular basis.

What distinguishes the telework center from the conventional branch office is that the people working in it are likely to have little or no organizational interdependence. Even if they work for the same company, they do not necessarily work together in the same group, department, or division. They are also distinguished from executive-suite offices—small office suites of less than a few thousand square feet intended primarily for small one- or two-person firms looking for an alternative to working from home where they can have access to shared secretarial services and office equipment. Telework centers, by contrast, are typically leased by larger firms that want to provide their employees with professional office space closer to their homes than a branch or central office.

ORGANIZATIONAL DRIVERS

Chief among the external forces for creating telework centers, particularly in the United States, have been state and federal environmental regulations mandating reductions in air pollution and traffic congestion and improved energy conservation. These regulations are forcing companies to rethink traditional work patterns such as the twice-daily migration of commuters in their individual automobiles.

In places as different as Finland and Kentucky, telework centers have also been promoted as a form of economic development. The intent in these cases is to exploit the potential of new information technologies to

The material presented here on telework centers is based in large part on a report by F. Becker, A. J. Rappaport, K. L. Quinn, and W. R. Sims, Telework Centers: An Evaluation of the North American and Japanese Experience. Ithaca, New York: Cornell University International Workplace Studies Program, 1993.

bring the work to an isolated rural workforce, rather than relocating people to urban centers.

A third driver behind telework centers has been an attempt by telecommunications companies like the Bell companies in the United States and NTT in Japan to exploit commercial gains from new technologies and associated business services. Telework center users, with their need to communicate with a central office and other telework centers, provide an ideal showcase for the new information technologies the telecommunications companies have developed. Telework centers in these cases become living laboratories and demonstration projects for products and services, as well as contributing to the overall image of the user company as being on the cutting edge.

Most organizations hope telework centers will also improve individual productivity. The assumption is that workers using telework centers will experience less stress due to shorter commutes, will have fewer interruptions during the work day, will have more flexible time options, and therefore will be able to work during their individual peak periods. In addition, performance is expected to rise because telework center users will have more time to spend with their families, reducing work-family stresses.

Evidence from a number of small, relatively informal, and unpublished case studies of telework centers in the United States (Quaid and Lagerberg, 1992), Canada (Finlay, 1991), and Japan (Spinks, 1991) suggests that many of the anticipated personal benefits for workers are being realized. As was true with home-based telework, the opportunity to work in a telework center can be empowering. It allows more freedom of choice about where and when one works. Workers reported that greater flexibility in work schedules allowed them to sleep more, reduced stress, and made it possible to spend more time with their families and participate more in community activities.

Immediate supervisors of telework center participants agreed that worker productivity was either maintained or improved. A key factor seemed to be that relatively fewer interruptions during the day allowed users to concentrate more on assigned tasks. Telework center users became more skilled at both time and project management. And because workers generally had access to the satellite facility twenty-four hours a day, seven days a week, many dropped in during off hours or worked longer than a typical day.

There were downsides, both for telework center users and their co-workers and supervisors. Many co-workers of telework center users voiced concern about being left behind—not surprising, since typically only a few selected workers were allowed to telework. When the pattern was to have workers use the telework center on a part-time basis, returning to the central office on alternate days each week, some managers felt that coordinating use of space, scheduling meetings, and keeping in contact with telework center users on a day-to-day basis became more difficult.

The telework center users voiced their own forms of separation anxiety. Some, particularly those in Japan, expressed worries about the potential impacts on their careers. They wondered whether being in a remote location either part or full time made them less visible to their supervisors and, thus, would cause them to be evaluated differently than their counterparts at the central office. The data on American teleworkers described earlier in this chapter suggests that, at least in this country, that concern may not be well founded.

One uniquely Japanese complaint was an outgrowth of spending more time at home. Telework center users became much more aware of—and dissatisfied with—the cramped quarters that characterize most Japanese residences. Many also felt guilty because they did not really know how to make productive use of their "spare time." Japanese users also commented frequently on the uncertainty in the chain of command and used words such as "bewilderment" to describe their experience with the self-management aspects of telework center environments.

U.S. and Canadian telework center participants, both workers and their immediate supervisors, spoke of the need for more and better training in alternative management techniques and work styles. Managers wanted more guidance on issues such as performance evaluation, maintenance of group synergy, and improving general communication. Workers echoed the desire for better communication links with both their supervisors and colleagues back at the central office.

These studies, as fragmentary as they are, suggest that telework centers do increase individual productivity. Yet in several cases a company's use of telework centers was discontinued when the pilot project officially ended. The obvious question is why, if telework centers seemed to work so well for staff and their managers, was their implementation not continued? The answer lies, we think, in the failure to convincingly demonstrate the potential for cost savings combined with the failure to seek a more effective way of working for the organization as a whole. This, in turn, is embedded in the failure to consider telework centers as a part of a larger integrated workplace system, rather treating it as a discrete alternative work pattern intended to accomplish a specific and narrow goal: reduce traffic congestion, improve air quality, or market new telecommunications products and services.

The Virtual Office

The concept of the virtual office goes a step beyond home-based telework, telework centers, and satellite offices. It refers to the idea that wherever one works is the workplace, be it a headquarters building, branch office, telework center, home office, or an airplane, car, boat, airline club, restaurant, or hotel lobby. Some intrepid New Yorkers have discovered that a well-appointed hotel lobby is a wonderful spot for meetings: comfortable chairs, quiet, easy access to food and drink, restrooms, and—with notepad and laptop computers with modem and fax boards, cellular telephones, and portable printers—all the information technology one could want. Even better, the "rent" for this prestigious location in one of the most expensive cities in the world is a few cups of expensive coffee and a generous tip.

THE ROLE OF TECHNOLOGY

Technology is a key ingredient in making the virtual office, and almost any form of remote work, effective. Access to voice mail and e-mail, to data bases and files from just about anywhere in the world, makes conventional time and space provisions for work obsolete.

Another key tool is the form of new software called "groupware," such as Lotus Development Corporation's LotusNotes, that enables individuals separated from each other to function as a group in real time. This will speed the breaking down of space and time boundaries still further. As we noted, Lotus is building its own new headquarters building using LotusNotes to link scattered members of the project team.

High-capacity video systems that just a year or two ago seemed like far-fetched futuristic toys are beginning to appear on desktops, and are likely to rapidly increase in number as the new generation of computers with video and multimedia capabilities come to market. These video capabilities are much more than just sophisticated picture phones. They create miniature "live boards" in which two or more people working thousands of miles from each other can work on the same document simultaneously. They can send, comment on, and modify the same photograph or graphic image. A project manager in Saudi Arabia can send video images of a building project to the firm's construction expert in Boston and they can discuss, in real time, the progress of the project in a way that is not terribly different than if the Boston expert had spent thousands of dollars and several days' time to fly to the actual building site. These kinds of distance-based multimedia systems are going to provide better opportunities for remote communication and interaction than the much more expensive videoconference rooms that were the only alternative just a few years ago.

REMOTE WORK AND SOCIAL INTERACTION

Despite an image many people have of remote work being socially isolating, not just in terms of work-related contact and communication but in terms of not being part of a meaningful social group, there is some evidence that the virtual office may actually broaden the range of face-to-face social contact, and even increase its spontaneity.

Howard Rheingold, in his book *The Virtual Community* (1993), describes people who have never seen each other becoming fast friends: helping each other out and rallying around to provide social support, advice, and a good ear in times of personal crisis. These are the kinds of behaviors we ascribe to effective communities, but often have a difficult time discerning when we look around our own neighborhoods. The difference in the virtual world is that the contact and communication may be with people outside our own work group or even our own company whom we meet as we move from place to place, both electronically and physically.

People working virtually are not locked up at home, but they may have enhanced opportunities to see and talk with other family and household members. They also meet with clients at the client's premises, and in hotels and restaurants. In many cases these are more pleasant, lively places to meet than the corporate office. They are also places to meet work colleagues, no longer confined to standing in a corridor or work station, having a cup of coffee in the break room, or meeting in the cafeteria.

Working virtually does not necessarily mean perpetual motion, or no home base. One may work in the same location for several days, and then switch to another as that makes sense, depending on the nature of the work being done or equipment and support needed. The key is that the employees design their pattern of workplace usage based on their own needs, tools, challenges, and opportunities, rather than fitting into some predetermined "best" structure. For those who seek and are willing to embrace this responsibility for choice, the virtual office tries to match work setting to work process in a dynamic way that recognizes and exploits the freedom to conduct work unconstrained by location.

CHAPTER EIGHT

Making Effective Use of Nonterritorial Offices

Larry, a sales representative for a large computer company, still comes into the main downtown office a few times a week, but now when he is in the office he sits at whatever work station he finds unoccupied. Michelle, a management consultant for one of the Big Six accounting firms, calls twenty-four hours in advance of coming into her office to reserve a work station. She, too, no longer has her own permanently assigned office or work station. Welcome to the world of nonterritorial offices.*

"Over my dead body." That's the way many people initially react to the idea of a nonterritorial office layout. For most of us, the most basic entitlement of working has been an assigned desk, work station, or office. No matter how small, dingy, dull, or uncomfortable the setup, at the very least we expected to have some place to call our own when we showed up for work. With everything from family photos and vacation pictures of the Grand Canyon to cartoons, achievement certificates, and stuffed animals, most of us tried to personalize the little bit of turf given to us by our employers. Until now.

But times are changing. Now companies like IBM, Ernst and Young, Andersen Consulting, Tandem, Amdahl Computers, General Electric,

Much of this chapter is based on work done by the Cornell University International Workplace Studies Program. For more details, see Becker, Davis, and Sims (1990), and Becker, Quinn, Rappaport, and Sims (1994).

AT&T, Bell Atlantic, and dozens more are saying to their staff, "You will have a good place to work when you are in the office, but because you are out of the office a lot of the time, the work stations will be used by different people." The surprise is that, first, for many people such offices are not terribly different from what they had before; and second, if planned and implemented well, such office arrangements can be as good as conventional assigned work stations or offices—if not better.

Driving Forces for Nonterritorial Offices

Whether called hoteling, nonterritorial, just-in-time, free address, group address, or shared office, the essence of the unassigned office approach is the same: the individual employee has no dedicated personally assigned office, work station, or desk. Rather, depending on the par-

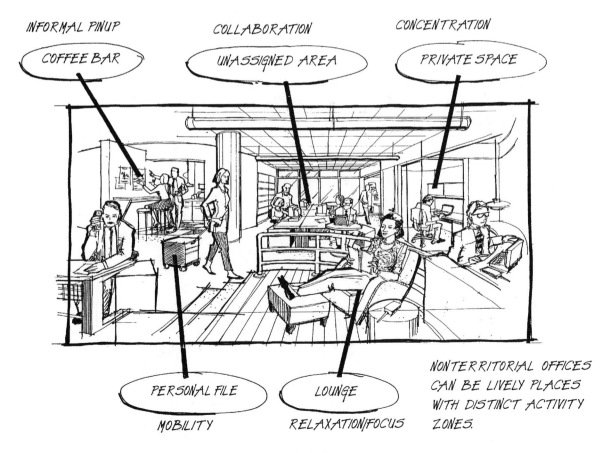

INFORMAL PINUP

COFFEE BAR

COLLABORATION

UNASSIGNED AREA

CONCENTRATION

PRIVATE SPACE

PERSONAL FILE

MOBILITY

LOUNGE

RELAXATION/FOCUS

NONTERRITORIAL OFFICES CAN BE LIVELY PLACES WITH DISTINCT ACTIVITY ZONES.

INTENSITY OF USE VARIES OVER THE DAY AND THE WEEK.

MONDAY MORNING

TUESDAY AFTERNOON

THURSDAY LATE EVENING

ticular system in place, people either call ahead to reserve an office or work station (called "hoteling" because of the similarity to making reservations at a hotel), or upon arriving simply take any available workplace that suits what they are going to do. In many ways this is a much more radical departure from typical office accommodation than working in a satellite office or telecommuting.

Most firms are committed to improving the productivity of their employees, and believe that anything that helps staffers such as management consultants, field salespeople, and customer service representatives stay in closer contact with their customers is likely to be helpful. Yet the primary driver behind nonterritorial offices for most organizations has been cost reduction. The reason is straightforward. In many companies expenses, especially those associated with real estate, have grown more rapidly than revenues over the past decade. When we combine those costs with occupancy studies that show that in jobs like field sales and management consulting employees typically occupy their office or work station only 25 to 40 percent of the time (a statistic remarkably stable across industries and countries), the value of using space better and with greater cost efficiency becomes very clear.

Nonterritorial offices accomplish this very well. Eliminating assigned offices makes it possible to accommodate the same number of people with fewer work stations. A common ratio is ten employees for seven work stations. The cost reductions associated with this kind of space intensification are very real.

The Many Forms of Nonterritorial Offices

Nonterritorial offices come in many different forms. They range from fully enclosed offices of 196 square feet overlooking San Francisco Bay to tiny work stations of less than 60 square feet. In many cases you would never even know you were looking at a nonterritorial office. In Ernst and Young's Chicago office, which uses a hoteling approach, when the management consultant arrives at her office she finds her name on the door and, if she wants, her family's photos on her desk.

A major defining characteristic of these primarily cost-driven approaches is that the work processes themselves have not been reengineered. The primary change is in what happens when you choose to work in the office—not in the nature of the work itself—in reward systems, in streamlining of business processes, or in organizational structure. Andersen Consulting's "just-in-time" nonterritorial offices in San Francisco, one of the earliest nonterritorial installations in this country, illustrate the benefits of a cost-driven approach very well.*

ANDERSEN CONSULTING'S JIT OFFICES

The branch office of Andersen Consulting in San Francisco occupied one floor of a high-rise tower in the financial district. Over time the practice, which focuses on helping clients develop, implement, and operate their data base systems, had grown considerably. If the firm continued its current space allocation practices, in which consulting managers were entitled to a 115-square-foot enclosed office, it would have to lease an additional floor.

The partner in charge of the office had observed in casually walking around the office that typically most of the assigned offices were vacant. In a partnership where increasing the number of billable hours is a prime consideration, the goal was to maximize the amount of time the consulting managers were out of the office and working directly with clients. Based on an informal assessment of actual occupancy patterns, the partner in charge then decided that some new working patterns should be implemented.

The partnership convened a committee of managers to address the problem of low occupancy and the need to accommodate more consulting managers while containing costs. The committee considered two options: assigning about five managers to each office; or developing what they came to call the just-in-time office system, in which a number of offices would be made available to the consulting managers to reserve in advance or use on a first-come, first-served basis if they came

*The Andersen Consulting case study, and the SOL case study reported later in this chapter, were done as part of two studies within Cornell University's International Workplace Studies Program (Becker, Davis, and Sims, 1990; Becker, Quinn, Rappaport, and Sims, 1994).

to the office unexpectedly. The managers preferred the just-in-time (JIT) system, since it eliminated potential conflict among people who would be assigned to the same office.

The primary goals of the JIT system were to:

- More intensively use space, given the low occupancy patterns.

- Reduce facility costs by reducing space requirements.

- Demonstrate to clients that they themselves were willing to put into practice new approaches to managing an organization.

The new JIT offices were based on the existing space standard; that is, some of the offices that had been designed for partners were now designated as JIT offices to be used by consulting managers on a reserved basis. The only difference between the JIT offices and partners' offices was related to policies about use; that is, the JIT offices are not personalized with family photos or individual mementos. Each office is furnished with a conference table that also serves as the desk. A credenza holds a telephone and computer and provides an additional work surface. The furniture in the JIT offices is identical to that in partners' offices.

Each consultant is assigned two file drawers and two binder bins in a centralized filing room. The distance between this room and the JIT offices ranges from 15 to 200 feet. Each JIT office also includes a number of commonly used standard reference materials, stocked and updated by support staff on a regular basis. A support person also stocks a standardized set of office supplies in exactly the same place in every JIT office.

All offices are equipped with a local area network. The major technological change from conventional practice was that each manager now has an individual telephone number, which is transferred by the secretaries to the office occupied at a given time. This necessitated installing many more phone lines than previously.

A small number of secretaries handle typing, reservations, and scheduling of the JIT offices. Managers call the secretary in advance to reserve a JIT office, or they can use whatever office is available if they arrive unexpectedly. A receptionist answers calls that are not answered by managers or secretaries, and also pages people and transfers calls. An additional staff person was hired specifically to stock the JIT offices and to ensure that all personal belongings and files were removed when the person using the office left. If all JIT offices are full, managers can use unoccupied partners' offices. Managers who reserve an office and then do not come in to use it lose their reservation if another manager needs the space.

Providing thirteen JIT offices for seventy consultants generated an annual rent savings of $114,000. Furnishing thirteen rather than seventy individual offices generated a total cost savings of $505,341 the first year. In the case of Andersen, the system easily accommodated change since partner offices could instantly be converted to JIT offices, and vice versa, without any physical changes. Moreover, the JIT offices emphasized a major management objective of encouraging consultants to get out of the office and spend more time with customers.

DOES IT WORK?

Employees' response to the Andersen JIT offices, as with other nonterritorial offices studied as part of the Cornell University *Workscape 21* research program, has been largely positive. Overall the JIT offices were considered slightly better than previous accommodation. Almost 90 percent of the respondents reported that the quality of the work done was about the same as previously, and about 70 percent indicated that the amount of work was about the same or better. While access to files and reference materials was rated as worse under the JIT approach by 75 percent of the respondents, the advantages of access to more sophisticated technology and the freedom to work whenever and wherever one wanted seemed to outweigh the disadvantages of not having extensive personal files at one's fingertips.

Similar results have been found in other nonterritorial installations that are still primarily cost-driven but have taken very different forms. IBM's version of nonterritorial offices in England, for example, uses a standard type of open-plan work station for its field sales representatives. Overall, the Cornell studies show that in most sites about 75 percent of the staff reported that the new office accommodation was as good as or better than their previous way of working. Given that the system has generated considerable cost savings, especially at larger sites, it is not surprising that interest in implementing nonterritorial offices has increased dramatically.

When we first started studying nonterritorial offices in 1989, the concept was considered extreme, if not bizarre. Most people, hearing about nonterritorial offices for the first time, were convinced they would never work. The companies we have studied therefore began exploring nonterritorial offices about three years ago with small pilot programs involving from twenty-five to sixty people. Most have now expanded these programs to involve hundreds and in some cases thousands of employees. Nonterritorial offices have become the standard form of office accommodation for all IBM UK and Canadian marketing and sales staff, for example, and more than twenty locations in the USA are now in the process of implementing their own versions. Ernst and Young has adopted nonterritorial offices in the United States and England, and Andersen Consulting has adopted them in the United States, England, and Japan.

Cost-Driven Versus Business-Driven

Without a doubt, nonterritorial offices can reduce costs, and if the technology and space provided genuinely support the work processes, employees will accept these kinds of offices. An alternative to the *cost-driven* model is what could be called a *business-driven* model. (We also discuss this in Chapter Twelve as cost-driven versus results-driven.) Companies using this model see the move to some form of nonterritorial office as primarily a means of improving overall organizational effectiveness and profitability. New workplace strategies in this context are carried out as part of an overall business reengineering process, with cost savings being a secondary, albeit appreciated, windfall benefit.

The productivity gain in business-driven cases comes from fundamental changes in organizational structure, performance measurement, and the business processes themselves. These kinds of organizational changes are facilitated by nonterritorial offices that promote informal and spontaneous communications among staff who sit in different locations each day, thereby widening their circle of contacts and friendships. Further mixing comes from space allocation policies that encourage and reinforce minimal status distinctions and disciplinary boundaries, easing the natural flow of information in the office. It also comes from managers operating under the same conditions as other employees, sharing the same space and resources, and thereby demonstrating their commitment to the new organizational patterns by modeling the desired and appropriate behaviors.

The difference between cost- and business-driven approaches is clearly reflected in the subsequent use of the space saved by having fewer offices. Cost-driven approaches tend to accommodate as many staff as possible in as small a space as possible. Little of the space saved is reinvested into other kinds of functional work areas, like dedicated project rooms and informal meeting areas. Even less is used to support diversity in work style that can help people be more productive, like using computers standing up or lying down, or incorporating dining and snack areas into the basic work area. Typically, in a cost-driven approach, some of the cost savings are reinvested in new information technologies, but these often are not used to significantly change the fundamental work processes. They just change the amount of work and when it is done.

A business-driven approach is more likely to take some of the space saved and reinvest it for missing environmental "tools" that the employees themselves have identified as important for improving their productivity. In Digital Equipment Corporation's British facility, this included shared spaces such as dedicated project rooms, better-equipped conference rooms, "quiet" rooms, and resource areas managed by a librarian.

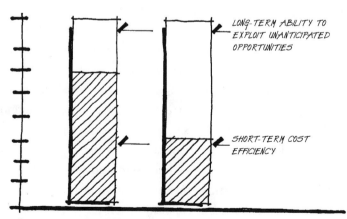

WHICH DO YOU PREFER: SAVED COSTS
OR LOST OPPORTUNITIES?

One of the best examples we know of a business-driven nonterritorial office approach is that taken by a Finnish cleaning company called SOL.

SOL'S BUSINESS-DRIVEN APPROACH

"You had better kill routine before it kills you." This is not the kind of statement one expects from a typical CEO, but then Liisa Joronen—and the company she heads—are hardly typical. For people looking for a model of how the planning, design, and management of the workplace can be used to support basic organizational values while enabling the firm to achieve its fundamental business objectives, SOL, a large cleaning company located throughout Finland, suggests some intriguing possibilities.

Company Background

SOL began operations two years ago when Liisa Joronen split off a business from the Lindström family, one of Finland's oldest and most prestigious family firms. Lindström had been testing many flexible management and workplace practices, including nonterritorial offices in the mid 1980s, before SOL was formed, but the family basically thought that many of Liisa's management ideas were too radical. When Liisa took the cleaning services aspect of the Lindström company separate to form SOL, she took with her several senior administrative people that she considered "progressive thinkers." She also inherited a workforce that in many cases had been with the family firm for twenty years or more.

Since it was launched SOL has also had to shift from operating in a super-heated economy in which, just a few years ago, Joronen argued that people will pay more for quality, to a marketplace that today demands quality at the lowest price simply as a condition of survival. SOL has, in this extremely tough, competitive marketplace, not only survived but thrived.

Management Practices/Philosophy

The bedrock of Joronen's management philosophy is that you must give your employees the opportunity to perform at their best. At SOL this means allowing office workers to work however they need to get the job done. This philosophy has driven a major reengineering of the company's basic business processes.

The traditional management structure, in which a few senior managers created budgets that staff were responsible for meeting by following detailed direction from management about the work activities, has been replaced at SOL by a structure in which managers of small cleaning groups are responsible for securing and serving their own clients. Supervisors of these groups set their own performance targets, budgets, and employee salaries. Where, when, and how they organize their work activities to meet the targets is largely at their discretion.

Because the margins are so tight in the cleaning business, detailed measurement of time, revenue, supplies, and so on is critical in order to constantly track profitability. Thus wide decision latitude and broad responsibility are balanced by complete dedication to measuring and improving performance. In practice, the goal of driving decisions and business responsibilities as far down into the organization as possible has resulted in the following kinds of management practices at SOL:

- Office workers have no prescribed working hours, and no written rules.

- There are no organizational charts, based on the principle that no person is any more important to the company than any other; the company cannot operate without the cleaners, the supervisors, the managers, and the administrators.

- All status symbols have been removed. No one, including Joronen or any of the senior managers, has an office, secretary, or any "special treatment." The company philosophy is that you earn respect through performance, not because of your organizational position.

- The administration at SOL is flat: no one has a job title. All workers have a particular area that they are primarily responsible for, such as accounting, bookkeeping, salaries, etc., but the expectation is that they will also spend a portion of their time doing other types of work. That is made necessary by the policy that when someone goes on vacation, another person must fill in during the absence. The goal is that when people return from vacation, they pick up on the work of that day, not where they left it.

- No information is considered secret within the organization. Figures on profits or losses, absenteeism, turnover, and so forth are distributed to employees in a monthly magazine. Individual performance is posted in the center of the office for all to see.

- The management system depends heavily on targets set by the employees. Targets are set one year in advance for each employee. The employees set their own targets, but they discuss these targets with their "supervisors" or "managers." Targets are composed of a number of separate performance indicators, such as sales, customer satisfaction, profitability, and the like. These targets and how well they are being achieved are not wholly private information. Selected targets and performances are currently posted on the "target tree."

- People are free to work how, when, and where they choose. The key factors that dictate how and when people work are the needs of customers, the people who actually pay everyone's salaries. Office workers also have internal clients whom they work for, whose expectations must also be met.

- Employees have both a fixed and variable salary, with the variable component (anywhere from 10 to 50 percent of the total) being based on reaching their targets (customer satisfaction, training, profitability, retaining customers, and so on). If they do not reach the targets set for the different factors, they do not get that portion of the variable component. Since a portion of the managers' target index is based on employee performance, managers and supervisors' salaries are dependent on the performance of their workers.

Training

We would expect that such a management philosophy and structure would require a strong commitment to employee training. At SOL this has taken, not surprisingly, a unique form. At a time when most people are cutting back on their training (the economy in Finland is at its worst point since World War II), SOL has increased its training levels.

Joronen initiated a SOL degree program composed of a series of five self-administered learning modules (training and instruction, public speaking, communication, productivity and work effectiveness, and SOL and services: the management philosophy), each developed by an outside consultant working with the staff. The entire program takes approximately two to three years to complete, with each module lasting anywhere from three to five months. Participation in the training programs is voluntary, but it is strongly encouraged.

In the service of furthering this fundamental reengineering of the business processes and structure, SOL's workplace strategy evolved, not as a junior partner, but as an integrated part of its business strategy.

Implementation Process

SOL's democratic, highly empowering philosophy was embedded from the beginning in the planning and design of the facilities, as well as the work itself. Small teams of five or six senior people initially narrowed the choice to four potential sites for the offices. Employees then had several opportunities to visit the different sites under consideration and to help choose the final location. The location that they chose had been a film studio, hence the name "studios" for offices.

Two design meetings were held, where everyone moving to the SOL studio was invited to participate in brainstorming sessions on how they wanted the office to look and function. People who were not able to attend the meetings could fill out absentee forms with their suggestions. Over a thousand ideas were collected, organized, and presented to an architect.

The architect then drew up preliminary plans for the overall office scheme using the ideas generated by employees. Employees reviewed the plans in four groups of about ten people each. Few of the staff liked the architect's original, quite traditional plan. They asked that he revise it, which he did, using the employees' suggestions. The space was fitted out in five weeks, with the staff pitching in to help prepare and paint the space. About twenty employees were actively involved in purchasing the furniture and other office accessories, although by the end of the process many employees had lost interest in this aspect of the process, leaving the architect to make decisions such as selecting task lighting.

Office Layout/Environment

The building, located in an industrial section of Helsinki, has "The City" as its central internal design theme, with a street (and street lights), building facades (residential, cityscape), blue night sky with stars, and a marketplace with a small fountain. There are twenty-five work stations for seventy employees.

Because employees were working in a nonterritorial environment before SOL was formed, the major difference in the new building is not in how space is assigned, but the dramatic change from conventional office furniture and subdued colors to a dramatic layout in a high studio space that offers a variety of work locations, from traditional work stations to highly distinct functional areas that have more the feel of a home than an office. These include areas like a patio to relax on with outdoor furniture, and a homelike dining room, living room, and kitchen. An exercise room is also available for employees.

A young children's playroom is provided for those employees who want or need to bring family members into the office. This area, equipped with a television, a stereo, and a video game system, is used primarily by the families when they accompany the employee to the office in the evenings or on the weekend. To brighten up the environment, stuffed animals are located throughout the office alongside live birds, mice, fish, and frogs.

Storage is handled in a number of different ways. A cityscape covers a wall of general historical storage that is approximately twenty feet high and thirty feet long. This storage is open shelving and contains a built-in ladder to allow access to the files. But at the time SOL was launched, the whole concept of filing and storage was rethought, and ultimately reengineered to eliminate more than 90 percent of the paper stored in the office. Each employee now has use of a small black cabinet located against the exterior wall, which contains two shelves. The other storage available to individuals is a large tote bag for holding their files and their post boxes. The majority of storage is done electronically, with the exception of the salaries and bookkeeping for which laws mandate hard copies.

A clean-desk policy is clearly in effect. People must clear the work station if they leave the office for any amount of time. People tend to use areas upstairs for team projects, for concentrative tasks, and for telephone calls requiring more privacy. The only smoking area in the building is a separate balcony with a very efficient ventilation system.

With its high ceilings, bright colors, residential furniture, dramatic circular windows, tentlike areas for supplies and mailing, and the sounds of birds and a fountain, SOL is like a dynamic miniature city, with its own electronic superhighway tools as well as places for working, eating, socializing, and recreation linked by the eye and the movement of people throughout the space over the course of the day.

Technology

Before SOL was launched, electronic diaries and calendars were in use at Lindström. In the new company, anyone who works flexibly (which is everyone except the cleaners) and wishes to have a computer at home (currently about 60 percent) is given one if they can justify the need. If a computer is not justified, portable computers are available to take home as needed.

Communications are handled in a variety of ways. Every employee in the office has a cordless telephone, and those who need one are also given a cellular phone for use outside the office. The employees have a direct number (for the cordless telephones) and all their calls to the direct number can be transferred to wherever they choose: home, car, voice mail, whatever.

In addition to the direct dial numbers, there is a main number into the Helsinki office. SOL does not, however, have any secretaries to answer these calls (secretaries are considered status symbols). Five telephones are located at different work stations, and people take turns answering them. Messages are written in a book and placed in people's individual post box if they are not in.

Employees have a computer system for looking up someone's telephone or fax number or e-mail address, and they can send messages using both voice and e-mail. People are in charge of letting others in the office know where they are so they can cover for or help people leaving messages. Interviews with staff suggest that it is actually easier to get in touch with people now because they are always accessible via car phones, home telephones, or e-mail.

Meetings are scheduled for the entire year so that employees know exactly when they must schedule to come into the office. Once a year the employees meet with their employers to set their targets for the year. They then have two meetings to determine if the targets are reasonable and if they are working well for them.

Organizational Benefits

SOL's new office cost a third of what it would have cost to implement a traditional office. This has nothing to do with nonterritorial offices, which were already in use, but with the use of residential rather than contract office furniture and an industrial rather than conventional office building.

More important, simple cost reduction was not the driving force—increasing market share and profitability was. The project's goal was to create a fun, lively, nonconventional office environment that employees liked, that they wanted to work in, and that supported the new ways of working Joronen initiated to help her company survive in a fiercely competitive business environment. According to Joronen, the building has played a central role in improving the lowly image of a cleaning company, which, as she says, "No one wanted to admit they worked for if you met someone on an airplane." Its main value, however, stems not from enhanced public image, but from the fact that the work environment itself is a constant, daily reminder to every employee that for SOL to survive it must innovate and continue to reengineer all of its approaches to work. The reengineering of business processes, which places so much emphasis on knowing what others are doing and how they do it, has, according to both Joronen and her employees, been significantly enhanced. The open environment and the physical accessibility of "managers" and others in the office possessing the skills for a particular task make it easier for people to ask for and quickly get the help they need to get their own work done, and to learn the essentials of others' jobs so they can step in when someone is absent.

The new facility, which communicates so directly and visually that SOL is not conventional, has also helped attract new staff. Even in a sluggish economy this is important in Finland, because the welfare safety net is so strong that cleaners and other lower-level staff can earn more from unemployment than from working. Yet SOL has a constant stream of people applying for work, something that will become even more advantageous as the economy improves. And because of the nonterritorial aspect of the space, Joronen estimates that she could increase the staff from 75 to about 110 people without making any changes in the current environment or adding any new space, thus reflecting considerable savings in space costs as well as the disruption of reconfiguring the office to accommodate new people. And in a business where customer satisfaction is absolutely essential and therefore measured systematically on a monthly basis, SOL's customer satisfaction ratings and the size and profitability of the customer base have steadily increased.

The driving force and ultimate test of SOL's approach is its success as a business venture. None of the changes in the environment were made solely for the sake of image, or merely to reduce costs. They were integral to Joronen's total business philosophy and the reengineering process she initiated to help the company prosper. For Joronen, the business itself could not operate as effectively as she envisioned it in a conventional office environment. Individual offices that encourage individual thinking rather than teamwork, walls that block easy learning of others' jobs, fixed positions that reflect time in the office as a performance measure rather than results, bland colors and minimal informal meeting and work areas that reinforce a business-as-usual attitude and discourage informal learning and sharing of information—all these are elements that Joronen believes are antithetical to a dynamic business. The environment here neither precedes nor follows the business: it *is* the business.

THE LONGER TERM ADVANTAGES OF BUSINESS-DRIVEN APPROACHES

SOL consciously and deliberately used the physical design and highly participatory planning and design processes for the workplace to encourage behaviors seen as critical to enhancing the firm's competitive edge. In doing so, SOL demonstrates how the thoughtful application of organizational ecology principles can contribute to a firm's long-term success.

Cost-driven approaches serve a useful purpose, obviously, but they are just that: an approach that must be justified in terms primarily of its real estate cost advantages. If those are absent or minimal, the approach has no other business justification. In smaller sites, or in locations where space costs are relatively low, justifying nonterritorial offices from a cost basis is likely to be difficult. In some cases, the additional cost of new information technology—laptop computers, modems, portable printers, more sophisticated telephone switches and services—may in fact outweigh the real estate cost savings, at least for several years.

The interesting point here is that money can be saved in both the cost-driven and business-driven systems, but productivity is much more likely to be enhanced in the latter. The most recent data from the Cornell University *Workscape 21* project found that the cases of business-driven approaches had significantly higher work effectiveness and satisfaction ratings than did cost-driven cases (Becker, Quinn, Rappaport, and Sims, 1994). Yet in both types of cases cost savings averaged around 20 to 30 percent.

Further, while the cost-driven approach requires a significant cost savings to justify it, which may be possible in a few larger installations but less so in smaller ones, the business-driven approach is potentially applicable throughout an entire organization, not tied to the size or location of its units. It is implemented because the new workplace strategy is a better way of working. In fact, some of the real estate cost savings gained from the larger sites can be reinvested in new technologies for smaller sites.

The Good Citizenship Versus the Performance Model

Regardless of whether the nonterritorial office is cost- or business-driven, a common feature is that performance assessment becomes more objective. Instead of measuring performance by time spent, in which good citizenship (coming in and leaving on time) is the hallmark of productivity, the focus shifts to actual results: what has been produced. It is very much like a university system. We have often heard students complain that they spent two weeks on a project, and received a *C*, while another student punched out the project in one long night and received an *A*. Under the good citizenship model, in which time is the measure of performance, this is certainly an unfair situation.

Under the performance model, it is eminently fair. What counts is what you do, not where or when you do it. We don't want to know how much time it takes a student to complete a project (we can't bill their hours to anyone), or what they are drinking, eating, smoking, or listening to while working, or what they are wearing, or who else is in the room. At best, knowing any of this is simply likely to make us nervous. What we care about are the quality and timeliness of the work. This approach is also beginning to invade corporate America.

Nonterritorial Offices: What's the Added Value?

For the individual employee, nonterritorial offices represent the loss of dedicated, personally assigned offices and work stations in a central office, but they do provide compensating benefits. These range from access to new information technologies that enhance productivity by making work easier and more efficient, to the opportunity to work in whole new workplaces that support individual choice about where and when to work. The loss of the ability to personalize your own work station or office, in this context, is replaced with much more powerful work tools and the opportunity to personalize your work not with family photos but with choices about when to come to the office and when to work at home or at a client's office.

All of these freedoms historically have been available only to the highest level of management, who came and went as they pleased. The intent with nonterritorial offices is to provide staff with the tools they need to work effectively, and then hold them accountable for high levels of performance. The nature of the "entitlement" shifts from ownership to access: people are entitled to have *access* to the space and equipment they need to get their work done.

For the organization, the value added by well-planned nonterritorial offices includes:

• Significant direct cost savings initially and over time.

• More intensive use of available resources such as space and equipment.

• A quality and quantity of work that are about the same as or slightly better than experienced with personally assigned offices or work stations.

- Depending on the nature of the design, greater potential for teamwork and group cohesion.

- Potential for enhanced public image with customers and clients as an innovative company.

The downside to nonterritorial offices lies in the risk of creating a sense of homelessness or anonymity among employees. This can be combatted by encouraging people to treat the whole place as their own.

This is the area in which offices like those at SOL are especially interesting. They have been able to shift the focus on spatial identity from the individual to the group. Unlike cost-driven nonterritorial offices, which are basically indistinguishable from the previous assigned offices, at firms like SOL the nonterritorial offices are part of a lively, unique, and truly personal place, not an anonymous corporate space. It is much more like a home in which there is a strong sense of family identity rather than a motel, with its strong sense of standardization and uniformity.

CHAPTER NINE

Developing an Integrated Workplace Strategy

Each of the new ways of working discussed in the previous chapters adds value in particular ways. However, none of these approaches by itself constitutes an integrated workplace strategy. Neither telecommuting, nonterritorial offices, nor any other single workplace solution can serve all workers or job functions or respond to all the pressures any organization is facing. The workplace needs to be treated as a system.

To achieve maximum benefit from implementing some form of workplace change often requires including other complementary changes. Leasing space for a telework center, for example, while maintaining the same array of individually assigned offices in a central location makes little sense in terms of occupancy costs and intensity of space use. It would be more sensible to create a strategy that from the beginning considers telework centers in conjunction with different forms of nonterritorial offices both at the central and satellite location, as well as part-time home-based telework.

The Cafeteria-Style Workplace

Integrated workplace strategies essentially require crafting a specific work pattern from an array of options. It is a bit like selecting a meal from a cafeteria line. Two people may create very different meals depending on how hungry they are, whether they eat meat or are vegetarians, how much time they have for lunch, and so on. In the context of the workplace, the appropriate combination of work locations, information technologies, and work processes is likely to vary depending on things such as the specific nature of the work being done, the stage in the project, or the experience of the employees. At early stages of a project a team may need to spend considerable time together, but the best place may be a quiet retreat rather than a conference room. Once the project is well underway and specific tasks are clear, working from home or a telework center a few days a week may be the best pattern, with the team meeting in an open but dedicated project space when they are in the office.

Like a cafeteria-style benefits plan, an integrated workplace strategy does not promise all workers anything they want. But it does recognize that people are different, and so are their work styles and optimal work patterns. From this point of view, the goal is to create different workplace options that can be selected by people doing the same job but who have different work styles, people doing different jobs, or even for the same people at different points in time as their personal circumstances change (for example, the birth of a baby, the need to care for an elderly relative, or an accident that makes commuting impossible).

Effective use of the organization's resources therefore lies not in the focus on an isolated alternative work setting but, as suggested in Chapter Seven, on the workplace as a series of loosely coupled settings. Individual settings—home, central office, telework center, hotel, client offices, automobile, airplane, and airport club—are conceived as part of a comprehensive workplace system. These varied work settings are linked by the physical movement of people and the electronic movement of information. The example of Digital Equipment Corporation's Finland office, described briefly earlier, captures this approach to an integrated workplace system exceedingly well.

DEC FINLAND

One could focus at DEC Finland on the nonterritorial aspect of the office, on its team office concept, on the use of home offices fitted out with computers and furniture by the company, on a company car equipped with cellular telephones, on access to customers' premises, and the use of hotels and restaurants while traveling. Yet none of these, by itself, captures what made this a truly integrated workplace strategy.

The key is that all of these elements were woven into a coherent system based on a clear understanding of work processes and a sense of how they could contribute to improving sales.

The intent was to redesign the nature of the work processes themselves so that sales representatives could spend more time with customers, orders could be made directly from clients' premises, sales representatives could respond to customer calls without delay, and communication among sales representatives serving different clients could be improved to facilitate coordination through the sharing of information and insights. There was no predefined schedule to dictate the use of these workplace elements; they were available for use as needed.

All of these settings were supported by advanced information technologies that included cellular telephones and sophisticated computer-based information systems accessible through local area networks and by modem using laptop computers. Another important element was the fact that the organizational culture valued performance (sales) over good citizenship (being in the office) and encouraged staff to choose when, where, and how to work most effectively. What gave form to the workplace system was not an abstract design aesthetic or a management edict to reduce costs. It was the intention to use all available resources to support the core business of the company: making a profit by selling as many computers and associated software and services as possible.

CHIAT/DAY

Another interesting case is the Chiat/Day advertising agency headquartered in Venice, California. The leaders recently declared the headquarters to be primarily a virtual office, with almost all the former residents (in both the creative and account management areas) no longer having dedicated assigned spaces in the central office.

Instead they are expected to consciously choose where they should be working each day, with a strong emphasis on being in the clients' territories and working at home. This is not simply a shift of venue, though—it is meant to be an integrated strategy. Laurie Coots, senior vice president for business development and project director for implementing their new "Team Architecture," described it very nicely:

"Our new operating philosophy has less to do with working at home than it does with not letting our work become 'geographically relevant.'

We want to make sure the value an employee can bring to the client is not limited by his or her need to be in the office. Therefore we have invested heavily in technology in order to bring the tools and collective intelligence of the office to the employee, regardless of their location. Conversely, the contribution an employee can make to the company is not dependent on 'keeping a chair warm' in the headquarters."

Such an approach inevitably creates more complexity; but it also strips away the pseudosimplicity of more conventional approaches that require people to work in a uniform way that often masks and undermines the diversity of work styles that could be harnessed to support greater organizational effectiveness.

NOVEX REVISITED

To get a sense of what this kind of integrated workplace strategy would feel like in a major American corporation, let's return to Novex, the slightly pseudonymous company profiled in Chapter Seven. Remember the dilemmas it was facing: how best to reduce costs, accommodate unpredictable change, manage control, improve building and employee performance, accommodate a workforce much more diverse in age, gender, and ethnicity, and exploit new communication technologies. Here is how an integrated workplace strategy worked for Novex.

The first realization was that no single approach would work. Top management made it clear that the organization was going to downsize in terms of both people and space. The question was not *whether* to do something radically different, but *what* to do.

Initially, a small telecommuting program was launched. Considerable care was taken to make it succeed. People were asked to volunteer, and those that did were closely screened in terms of their job function, home situation, personality profile, and supervisor support. From the volunteer group a small number of people in the sales group were selected. They received two days of training, and the company installed a work telephone line, computer, modem, and office furniture in their homes. Most of them actually only work at home two or three days a week. The other days they are back in the central office.

Since they are in the office only two to three days a week, and not always on the same day, their use of work stations is now different. They have access to work stations identical to those they occupied before, but not necessarily the same ones. A ratio of six work stations for ten people was implemented, and, except for a brief period on the occasional Monday mornings, no overloading of the area has occurred so far.

The program worked well for the staff who participated. Publicizing the program helped the organization strengthen its image as a cutting-edge firm concerned about its employees' welfare. The problem was that the number of employees involved was very small.

The next step was to introduce the nonterritorial office concept on a much wider scale throughout the sales organization. First a simple occupancy survey was conducted over the course of a month. The data showed, to everyone's surprise, that most offices were unoccupied from 60 to 70 percent of the time. People were in meetings, on the road, or at a client's workplace.

As part of the systematic assessment of actual work patterns, which had never been done before, Novex found that large numbers of its staff were spending six to eight hours a week in airports. It also learned that while a significant percentage of people were interested in working a few days a week at home, there was also a sizable number who felt they could not work effectively at home: too many distractions, no extra space, the desire to separate home and work life, and so on. But these same people also complained about long, stressful commutes and time lost in the central office because of distractions and interruptions.

Focus groups, interviews, and survey data revealed one further widespread problem: despite Novex's high-tech image, almost 75 percent of the surveyed staff reported that the technology they were using was outdated. While a few laptop computers were available to be checked out, the demand exceeded the supply. People who wanted to work at home or even just at different company locations had difficulty working together because the company had not provided currently available software that could help, for example, in the remote editing of task reports. Even for the software that was provided, there was often inadequate training and support in how to use it, and particularly in getting immediate help when a problem occurred.

The picture painted by this new information was fairly bleak: the company was paying a lot of money for space that was often unoccupied; people were not as effective as they felt they could be when they were in or out of the office; and they spent a lot of time commuting that was stressful and nonproductive. The large number of staff commuting also made it difficult for the company to meet government-mandated targets for the number of trips per employees per day.

The telecommuting program, while positive, had not really improved the basic work processes, nor was it saving the company much space.

At this point a much more integrated workplace strategy began to be developed. The starting point was not reducing costs. It was rethinking how work was being done and creating organizational, technological, and workplace solutions that supported the way work could be done most effectively. The new workplace strategy was built on four fundamental and completely new premises:

1. *Support rather than deny the diversity* that existed in the workforce. The survey data showed conclusively that even people doing the same job did not have the same lifestyle or work style. Some people worked well early in the morning, others late at night. Novex found that employees with young children were not as eager to work at home regularly as had been expected, while those without children appreciated being able to work at home where it was often easier to concentrate.

2. *Consider small but important differences in work process* between jobs that had the same title and had up to then been treated as identical. For example, field sales staff whose customers were primarily large companies turned out to travel much less than those whose clients were small organizations. Equity was now defined as providing people with the supports they needed to get their job done, not providing everyone with the same thing. This was accomplished by having all employees write up a one-page business case justifying the equipment they needed to work effectively. People who traveled frequently to visit small clients requested cellular telephones and laptop computers. Those working from large clients' premises were less interested in cellular telephones. Those who frequently traveled by air justified airline club memberships. This policy, which previously would have been considered unfair (since everyone at the same level doing the same job didn't get the same thing) now made sense, and it enabled the company to allocate its scarce resources where they would do the most good.

3. *Treat the cost of new technology as an indispensable business expense.* Furthermore, technology needs would now be assessed in terms of

the extent to which they supported diversity—that is, enabled people doing different jobs as well as people doing the same jobs but with different work styles or family situations to have the technology that helped them to be productive. The cost of this technology was substantial—millions of dollars in one year—but that represented a relatively small percentage of salaries and wages. More to the point, without the right technology the workplace and work process strategies intended to improve overall organizational effectiveness could not be successful.

4. *Generate new team and individual performance measures based on specific task accomplishment.* No longer was good citizenship, such as showing up early and going home late, taken as evidence of productivity. Employees were given the tools they said they needed to work effectively, clear targets were agreed upon by employee and supervisor, and then performance was accurately measured.

With these principles, Novex began what was essentially a series of negotiations with employees to learn how they felt they could work most effectively: where did they want to work, what communication tools did they need, what were the best ways to measure performance? The company also provided educational sessions to its staff to increase awareness about the new principles and to provide employees with new ways of thinking about how they could be most effective.

At the same time, the range of ways of working offered to staff was greatly expanded. New technology, most immediately laptop computers with high-speed fax modems and portable printers, was made available to those who could make a business case for needing them. Using a docking station, people who used laptops outside the office could easily plug into larger screens and full-sized keyboards when they worked in the central office. Voice mail that could be accessed from any telephone anywhere was made available to all employees.

Novex established several types of satellite workplaces. In some cases they leased space in small telework centers in areas where high concentrations of employees lived. In other cases they were able to orchestrate a space swap: a firm that had surplus space in an area where Novex employees lived made that space available to Novex, and Novex did the same with its own surplus space for the other company. Thus more (and handier) work locations were created without having to lease additional space. Work stations in these centers were available by reservations or drop-in: no assigned offices existed.

In large parts of the headquarters office people whose work or work style was best supported by coming to the central office each day did so, but the office they occupied was now a uniform, compact ten-by-ten-foot space. Everyone's personal storage was reduced by a minimum of 30 percent. Eliminating the personal reference libraries of each employee, which tended to have about the same basic material, and creating a managed set of distributed reference materials, helped considerably. So did the transfer of reference and support materials from hard copy to electronic data bases.

Those who came to the central office occasionally now used a non-territorial work station when they were in the office. They were also encouraged to work in small group rooms with desks but no surrounding panels, so they would be more likely to see and talk with other people when they were in the office.

Recognizing how much time Novex people spent in air travel, company leaders made executive club memberships available for those who traveled more than fifty days a year. For those who spent more time driving, cellular telephones were provided.

The net result of all these changes has been to transform the nature of how business is conducted at Novex. Each individual has far more personal freedom, and much greater responsibility. Control is now exercised not through edicts about where and when and with what tools people must work, but in terms of what they produce. It is not a comfortable place to coast, but it is an exciting place to work.

The difference for the employees is dramatic. Consider what happened for Edith and Jim, two typical Novex employees. Before all these changes, both of them rose every morning about 5:30 and then left for work about 6:30. Edith drove, a grueling ninety-minute commute made worse in the winter when the roads were often covered with snow or ice. Jim drove to the local commuter train station and then rode to work on the train, usually dozing or reading the morning paper.

When they got to work, both went to their offices, hung up their coats, and dropped off their briefcases. Then they got coffee, chatted with others getting coffee, and went back to their office, where they checked their e-mail and voice mail. Then Jim was off to meetings for most of the morning, dropping back to his office between meetings, mostly to catch his breath, glance over a report, or meet with a staff person for a few minutes. Then, back to meetings. The basic pattern repeated itself after lunch and each day. Edith typically spent the morning writing reports, in between phone calls. She left the office in the afternoon to visit clients, either checking back into the office at the end of the day for messages, or just going home from the last client.

Things have changed. Edith gets up an hour later, dresses, and then goes into her home office. Using her telephone she checks all voice messages; with her computer and modem she checks for e-mail, replying to both immediately. She writes reports without interruption until about 11:00 A.M., when she walks to a neighborhood work center about two miles from her home. The walk takes about half an hour, and Edith loves both the exercise and the fact that she actually gets to the office much faster than her minimum commute used to take. When she has meetings with clients, she meets them at the neighborhood work center, which is also where she meets with those staff who live in her area.

A few times a week she drives to the main office at off-peak hours, when the roads are less congested, where she has lunch with staff and catches up on news and office gossip. Then it is off to clients. In between client visits she visits a favorite coffee shop where she updates reports on her laptop. She sometimes then comes back into the office around 5:30 P.M., and works there in a nonterritorial office until about 6:30, when she drives home, having missed much of the rush-hour traffic.

Jim still catches the morning train. He finds it difficult to work at home, and besides most of his work is meeting with other people. When he gets to work he goes to his small private office, which is outfitted with a desk, a computer, voice mail and e-mail; he works here between face-to-face meetings. All meetings are held in a set of conference rooms that can be scheduled directly from the computer in his office. The conference rooms are fitted out with VCR and video conferencing equipment, overhead and slide projectors, and easy-to-use multimedia tools. With these tools he can view, interact with, and edit presentation materials, which incorporate data in the form of graphs, narrative text, video clips, and written text.

An electronic white board and large screen connected to the computer equipment allow whatever has been generated on the computer to be viewed by all present in a large, highly visible format. Special "groupware" software allows the different participants in the meeting, and increasingly other task team members who are located all over the country, to edit what is being produced in real time. All of the information produced can be directly conveyed to management for review, including members of the European subsidiary who have partial responsibility for the project. The result is that at the end of each meeting a totally accurate record of the meeting is available. Even material that was scrawled by hand has been converted to type so that everyone can read everyone else's notes and comments. At the point where final decisions are made, the final presentation materials can be quickly generated.

Two people, two jobs, two different ways of working. In the old work structure, the workplace masked the differences, forcing each into a pattern that was unproductive, inefficient, or both. Now, with unassigned offices in both satellite space and in the main office, the space costs saved have been reinvested in new technology and a wider range of workplace supports, including airline club memberships and the telework centers. The organization's flexibility is high, since it can terminate the short leases in the telework centers without much penalty. Because they are being used by people living in these locations, and home locations change less frequently than job assignments, telework centers make sense even when the organization changes.

The new workplace system is more complex to manage, but computer systems make it easy to track and monitor what space is owned and leased. Because users log on to computers in different locations to have their phone messages automatically forwarded, Novex can easily and automatically track the frequency with which offices and office locations are being used. This information helps in making decisions about the value of different site locations and of different policies and practices for allocating space and equipment. The computers are now working to support diversity.

Changes Required for an Integrated Workplace Strategy

For integrated workplace strategies to succeed, organizational leaders must concern themselves with the following issues:

1. *System interdependency.* Changes in one part of the system will affect other parts. Making available telework centers, for example, means that the original office accommodation in a central or branch office should change, as should the provision for working at home. This, in fact, is what IBM has done with what it calls its "mobility program." Field sales staff now can work at home, in offices equipped with IBM furniture, computers, and telephone lines; at their customers' premises, using their laptop computers and printers; in their car with cellular telephones; and in nonterritorial office settings at what IBM calls its "productivity centers."

A change in one part of the system, the decentralization of work away from a central office, has changed the nature of all the other settings that are part of the workplace system. Most individual employees have no workplace they "own," other than their home office (which they may also share with family members), but they have an array of settings in which they can choose to work, based on their own determination of which place makes the most sense for the task or activity.

2. *Changing expectations.* For many managers and employees, "real" work is sitting in front of a computer or being in a scheduled meeting. Management and staff both need to change their expectations about what each should be doing when working at a telework center, at home, in a nonterritorial or team office, or at a customer's premises. When people are in the central office, enlightened management would want to see them talking with each other, sharing information, catching up on news. This should be considered real work, not time out.

3. *The right technology.* Taking advantage of new ways of working requires exploiting new information technologies. Laptop computers equipped with high-speed fax modems would be the standard issue rather than the exception, so that one computer is associated with each person and that person can work in any number of locations. The ratio of more sophisticated printers in the office could be reduced, while the number of portable printers would be increased. The same would be

true with fax machines. Whatever technology is provided should be upgraded as significant breakthroughs occur, and replaced long before it has become a dysfunctional piece of old iron.

4. *Education and training.* New ways of working are fostered by providing management and staff with training about how to work in a variety of locations: organizing their time, using new technology, choosing where to be, and sensing problems at an early stage and resolving them. Initially managers and staff will need regular opportunities to express their concerns, to quickly obtain help in resolving unexpected and new problems, and to be reassured that the organization's goal genuinely is to help everyone become more productive, not just to slash costs.

Getting these kinds of support programs and policies in place, and getting them right, is critical. One organization we know initially thought the best way to do this was to provide a few days' training on how to use the new software and hardware, and then to charge employees each time they called asking for any information that had been covered in the training session. In effect, employees were going to be penalized for not learning or remembering everything they needed the first time through. This seems completely counterproductive to us. The idea is to make employees feel comfortable getting the training and computer service they need, not to discourage them from asking for help.

A more imaginative approach is being considered by Sprint, the telecommunications company. It has conceptualized service support in a way that is similar to luxury automobile manufacturers. If you experience a problem, there is a twenty-four-hour hot line to call for assistance. You can bring your computer in for repairs in exchange for a loaner, or you can send your computer in overnight mail to the repair center and get a loaner back the same night, with the same software as the one you sent in, so that no working time is lost.

5. *Performance assessment.* With new freedoms come new responsibilities for everyone. As people work more remotely, or even just in different ways, more information must be collected about individual, group, and organizational performance, especially in terms of how these affect the customer. At SOL, the Finnish cleaning company discussed in Chapter Eight, this took the form of monthly customer surveys, rating the quality of service. Other firms regularly call a random sample of cus-

tomers and ask them to comment on the speed and quality of service they have received. Many companies automatically track how long it takes for telephones to be answered as one measure of customers' experience with service.

Along with more trust by management that employees who are not physically present are really working, there must be acceptable performance indicators, agreed upon by management and staff, to assess productivity and effectiveness. As an example, consider the prototypical knowledge-work organization, the university.

The research staff of the International Workplace Studies Program, which Professor Becker leads, meets every Monday to agree on performance targets for the coming week. The intent is to set targets that are challenging but attainable. This might include agreeing to do ten interviews, write a draft of a chapter, format a report, complete a data analysis, and generate new graphics. Each Monday progress on the previously agreed targets is also reviewed. Not meeting a target now and again is understandable. Consistently missing targets triggers an examination of the reasons or problems behind the misses.

The point of the targets is to create an objective set of performance goals that can help guide work wherever people choose to do it. Trust has to do with when and where the work gets done, not with *whether* it gets done. That can be measured. There has to be a clear understanding that management's responsibility is to provide the necessary tools, training, and guidance; the employee's responsibility is to get the job done.

6. *Employee participation.* Getting the technology, the design, and the use and allocation of both of these right requires directly involving staff in discussions about how they can work most effectively. As we will discuss in Chapter Ten, there are many techniques for doing this, from surveys and focus groups to intensive design workshops. The process must not simply solicit information about work patterns, but involve staff in developing, reviewing, and approving proposed design and technological solutions.

7. *Process versus solution approaches.* There is another dimension related to employee participation that has broad implications for rolling out a new workplace strategy across the entire organization. It has to do with what one chooses to standardize. In some organizations, once the pilot

phase for some new workplace option—a nonterritorial office, say—is completed, the goal is to stamp out in cookie-cutter fashion virtually identical workplace solutions from one location to another. Research findings from the Cornell International Workplace Studies Program suggest that this does not work very well. Field sales staff in California may have the same job title and responsibility as field sales staff in New York City, but the conditions under which they work, the location and size of their customers, patterns of work in the local culture, and the regulatory environment in which they must operate may all be quite different.

Companies like Ernst and Young and Amdahl Computers have recognized this, and have chosen to standardize the principles and processes used to create innovative new workplaces, not the specific solutions themselves (Joroff and Becker, 1994). Thus Ernst and Young's Chicago office bears little resemblance to the New York office, and what happens in Montreal is different from what happens in Toronto. What drives these approaches is a common process that emphasizes management setting the boundaries and constraints on such things as the amount of space or funding available and then giving employees the opportunity to use their imagination to create a workplace that matches their needs within these boundaries.

8. *Organizational leadership.* New ways of working cannot be effectively developed and implemented without genuine involvement and commitment on the part of the organization's leaders. There must be an articulated vision that guides the development of the specific strategy. New ways of working are not just a technical or administrative consideration. They strike to the heart of the organization's culture, its most deeply rooted values about the way things should be done, people should be treated, and leadership should be practiced.

Changing the Culture Is the Goal

Cost-driven approaches to new workplace strategies tend to focus on a single new way of allocating space, such as nonterritorial offices, or on new work locations, such as telework centers or the home office. Changes in the culture happen, but they are an outgrowth, a kind of necessary evil, of doing essentially the same job but in different places and perhaps at different times. As the Novex example suggests, integrated workplace strategies are more likely to start from a desire to change the culture and structure of the organization as well as the work processes themselves. In such business-driven approaches, changing the culture is the goal, not a byproduct of a change in how space is allocated. Developing an integrated workplace strategy requires a paradigm shift, a new culture with a new set of attitudes, values, and organizational relationships.

The benefits of such an approach are considerable. Organizations will be better able to attract diverse staff, to reduce costs while enhancing adaptability, and to enhance teamwork and individual productivity while improving both quality of work life and home life. Ultimately, workplace strategies can become a win–win program not just for the individuals and their managers, but for the organization concerned about using its available resources to their fullest potential.

In Part Two we will examine the planning processes, leadership roles, resource allocation strategies, and guiding assumptions that foster integrated workplace approaches and ultimately a healthy balance in the ecology of the organization.

PART TWO

PUTTING SPACE TO WORK

CHAPTER TEN

Up-Front Planning: Launching a Vision-Driven Workplace

Americans are action-oriented. For many managers nothing seems more like a waste of time than discussing and debating the processes that will be used to plan a course of action or reach a decision. We encounter reluctance about this all the time in our work as consultants helping organizations create more effective workplaces. Even when the project's leaders think they have spent sufficient time creating an effective process, they often have not. Designing processes that involve all relevant stakeholders—architects, engineers, interior designers, project managers, corporate managers and executives, and staff—in a way that secures their commitment to the project and elicits from them the necessary information and opinions is a major design project in its own right—one that is too often given short shrift.*

Good intentions are often confused with good execution. In one particular case we worked with, the manager invited fifty staff members to sit, lecture-style, in a three-hour "feedback" meeting as part of a corporate project to experiment with new workplace designs. This reflected genuine interest in communicating with staff but did not generate enthusiasm for the project or elicit high-quality information about the

*Parts of this chapter originally appeared in F. Becker, "Adding Value Through Process Management," Industrial Development, Dec. 1993, pp. 1395–99.

staff's views. People are often reluctant to speak up in a public setting, especially if they are not sure how the information will be used or what is expected of them. In effect, contrary to the project manager's intent, the meeting became a "feedout" process, in which the project team members discussed their own experience and ideas, with minimal feedback from staff.

As the session dragged on, and the staff did not respond, the manager began to get frustrated. Sitting at the rear of the room, with the staff facing away from him, he tried to prod the group into talking about privacy and what they felt about "shared offices." Was this something they thought they would like or could live with?

Gradually it dawned on us that in the project manager's mind the data collection that had occurred with staff as part of an associated research project *was* the design process. He felt the process had dragged on for months (ever since the research began), and that there was little to show for it in terms of concrete action: that is, new design concepts. For him, this meeting was to "get it done." His goal was to get the feedback from staff in the morning, and decide on the design in the afternoon.

This meeting exemplified much of what can go wrong in planning and designing the workplace. Everyone was confused about the goals of the meeting, and certainly no consensus had been reached—because there had been no debate in early stages of the planning process—about how the design process should proceed. The process itself was not stimulating excitement in staff or project planners, and in terms of elapsed time the project was dragging on.

In truth, the design of a new team environment for a group this size could have been done very efficiently, in about a week's time. But this would have required taking the time to carefully structure the process: knowing exactly what kind of information to collect, shaping how the information could be collected efficiently and effectively, creating quick turnaround feedback loops between data collection and preliminary designs, and so on. It also would include taking the time to make sure everyone involved in the process, as planners or users, understood the goals, objectives, and various stages of the project, and where they fit into them.

Blocks to Effective
Planning Processes

There are several reasons why corporations are not terribly good at using effective planning processes. For one, our colleges and universities tend to be poor at teaching process-management skills. Many business schools hardly involve students in team projects requiring communication and collaboration; the emphasis is on competition and individual achievement. As a consequence, we underestimate the value of teamwork.

We see the results in our own students. The Americans tend to compete, while Japanese and European students like working in teams and are less likely to confuse effectiveness with getting one's own way and beating down the others in the group. Successful teams by their nature require consideration of process: who will be the leader, how will decisions be made, what information should be collected, how will conflicts be resolved?

Effective teamwork in workplace planning calls for members to consider each other's values and work styles. We need to confront conflicting views that can be as professional and legitimate as our own, all the while accepting the unbounded idiosyncratic nature of the human race whose personal mannerisms, health, dress, and language can amaze, bewilder, frustrate, annoy, infuriate, amuse, and delight us. In other words, working with people can be very tough. It can also be wonderful, but it takes skills and attitudes that many of us sorely lack.

A second factor is the tendency of action-oriented leaders to equate results with tangible "things," whereas in many situations, process can be the most important product. Studies of how organizations progress from small pilot projects to corporatewide programs involving the implementation of nonterritorial offices as part of Cornell University's *Workscape 21* project have shown, for example, that the success of such programs is most dependent on the planning process. Increasingly sophisticated and refined workplace designs and better technology did not, in these studies, correlate with either more staff satisfaction or greater work effectiveness (Becker, Quinn, Rappaport, and Sims, 1994).

A third block to effective planning processes is the tendency of organizational leaders to jump to solutions for space problems without an adequate diagnosis. Realizing that something different needs to be done is a good first step, but the frequent practice of jumping from that point to discussions of how to implement what is assumed to be a good solution can be a prescription for wasting time, energy, and money.

For example, we recently received a call from an executive of a high-tech company in California. The senior managers of this company had realized that their existing approach to space planning, more or less a standard open-plan layout with all the systems people tucked into a rabbit warren–like maze, had become dysfunctional. The problem occurred with the next step in the thinking process. They quickly decided that furniture was the key issue, and then proceeded to commission a thorough analysis of the wrong thing: which furniture system to buy.

They thought of themselves as being in an analytical phase of the project when, in fact, they had already jumped to a solution based on furniture rather than, possibly, policies and norms governing how the existing space could be used. Or the problem might have been the basic configuration of the building, or the nature of available information technology, or the question of where different groups were located in the building. Or, more than likely, the problem stemmed from the interaction of several of these factors. Asking and getting answers to these kinds of questions are likely to lead to a much broader range of solutions than this company actually considered.

Why would managers move so quickly from awareness that some aspect of the workspace is dysfunctional to choosing a new furniture system? One reason may be that furniture is a familiar focus for many managers. The issue can be treated as essentially a procurement problem, for which there are already accepted methods and procedures. This triggers a detailed and focused analysis. If more fundamental questions were being asked about organizational vision, direction, and culture, the analysis would be more exploratory and the nature of the conclusion less certain, possibly more threatening. Jumping to furniture as the solution avoids these bigger questions that don't have easy answers.

TAKING THE TROUBLE TO DO A THOROUGH UP-FRONT ANALYSIS

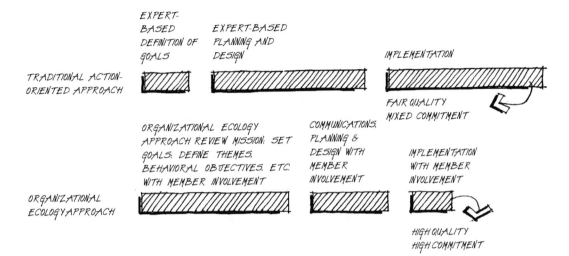

Clarity About Direction: Taking Care in Early Steps

In this same company questions could also be raised about whether there was a clear sense of agreement at the top about strategic directions, particularly regarding new ways of working. Management had not held discussions about a range of basic organizational and management issues, such as more teamwork and collaboration, more emphasis on informal communication, less autocratic management styles, more responsibility and authority given to individuals and work groups. There didn't seem to be a consensus about these issues, nor was there a clear philosophy about the role of the facilities as they related to and supported the organization.

Managers too often feel they should move forward quickly, both to meet schedules and to keep costs down. Yet, inadvertently, they may end up spending a great deal of effort, money, and time to do something that isn't necessarily going to improve the organization's competitive position much in the long run. While some problem is likely to be solved, it may not be the right one.

The long-term disadvantage for the organization is that the process itself is not likely to reveal the shortcomings of the action orientation. Typically, when the solutions (often to a minor or wrong problem) do not generate the expected results, the easy—and wrong—conclusion is that the design, planning, and management of the workplace really aren't important factors. This is a form of blaming the victim.

While we have come to understand that there are lots of flaws to the Japanese decision-making process, one aspect of their process that continuously perplexes Western, and especially American, managers is how it is possible to spend so much more time in planning stages, and at the same time shorten the product development cycle. The answer lies, to a large extent, in employees' commitment to the decision. American managers, preoccupied with getting something done, tend to make decisions quickly, before they are properly thought through and certainly before everyone required to implement them understands and agrees to the chosen course of action. In the Japanese process, once the considerable effort in the planning stages has resulted in a decision, there is no looking back. All effort moves ahead with great speed and single purpose. It's a great example of the "both/and" approach to decision making: planning *and* speed, rather than the false dichotomy of choosing between planning and speed.

Spending the necessary time up front is critical if the goal is identifying the real issues so that whatever time and money are available can be used to their fullest potential to actually solve real problems. A pharmaceutical firm constructing an R&D campus asked us to help decide whether the cafeteria should be full or partial service, and located in one building or another. This was a reasonable project issue. But it was also a relatively unimportant question when the major challenge facing the organization was getting new products into the marketplace faster. The main barrier to a faster product development process was the physical separation of the discovery research people from the development people who were responsible for transforming an idea into a commercial product.

The key organizational problem in this case was, in fact, how to create facilities that would facilitate true collaboration between the research and the development people. Given the difference in laboratory requirements and work styles, as well as the negative stereotypes and attitudes that often separate these groups socially and professionally, this was admittedly a much thornier issue, a genuinely wicked problem that would take more time and effort than deciding where to locate the cafeteria. But an innovative answer—inventing a combination of new facilities designs and new working practices that could overcome the conventional barriers in the pharmaceutical research process—had the potential to move the company a quantum leap forward.

A true reworking of an organization's work style and workplaces can't occur unless at least a couple of high-powered, high-credibility executives feel strongly that it should happen and are willing to put time, attention, and public commitment behind an honest problem diagnosis. When such people decide to take the lead in key facilities issues, real diagnosis can take place. Without them, the conventional facilities questions get asked (cost per square foot, churn rate costs, how to control the workforce's chaotic tendencies) but they don't result in very much change in terms of matching workplace choices to long-term organizational directions.

Crucial Up-Front Planning Steps

When creating a new work setting (headquarters, laboratory, field center), most organizational leaders tend to essentially recreate whatever is being replaced, except making it larger, cleaner, newer, in a different location, or with upgraded supporting technology. The new setting often requires people to work in pretty much the same ways that they did in the old one.

However, every major physical facility project presents an opportunity to do much more. It is a natural point to update people's sense of the organization's mission, to define needed changes in how the system should work in order to achieve that mission, and to identify key principles for workplace design and management that will achieve the system's business and organizational objectives. In other words, this physical change, if managed consciously, is an opportunity to reinvigorate the organization.

To fulfill this potential, leaders need to build a sort of "Phase Zero" into their process: a series of direction-setting steps that precede and set the context for the later stages, which most people think of as the real process. Phase Zero is just as important as any of the later stages, since it affects everything that follows it. To do it well you must first clarify a shared vision for where you're going, what the workplace is intended to support, and therefore why it is being shaped as it is.

For this shared vision to be created, the organization's leaders have to

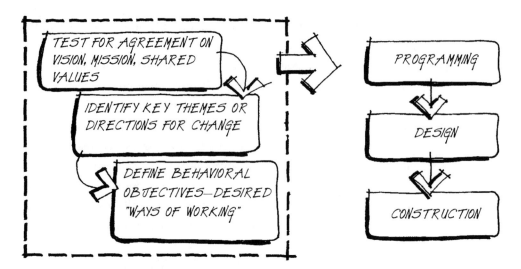

TEST FOR AGREEMENT ON VISION, MISSION, SHARED VALUES

IDENTIFY KEY THEMES OR DIRECTIONS FOR CHANGE

DEFINE BEHAVIORAL OBJECTIVES—DESIRED "WAYS OF WORKING"

PROGRAMMING

DESIGN

CONSTRUCTION

KEY "PHASE ZERO" STEPS FOR A PLACE PROJECT

get involved before the more traditional programming process establishes parameters for the project such as size and technology requirements. If this up-front work is done well, it serves as a reference point for all the programming, design, and construction that follow. There are several parts to it.

1. *Review the organization's mission and core values*, so that there is agreement about who you are, what you're trying to do, and how you want to do it. This includes emphasizing any changes that are desired in this area.

2. *Identify a manageable number of key requirements or "themes" for the project.* One company we worked with (Company A) identified two key business goals for a new building project: to produce more creative products, and to reduce by more than half the development time between the conceptual stage and bringing a new product to market. These key factors were chosen as most likely to determine the future success of the organization. Another client (Company B) defined its goals as building and maintaining high-quality relationships with customers and suppliers, developing a strong intelligence capability (rapid gathering, sharing, and interpretation of information), ingenuity in identifying new business opportunities, and ability to respond quickly to changes in the company's environment (markets, supplies, politics, economics, and so on).

3. *Develop a set of behavioral objectives or desired ways of working.* In essence this is an explicit statement about how you want individuals,

groups, and the whole organization to function in the new environment. It is especially important here to specify any desired changes or change directions from the way people currently do their work. From Company B's mission and key themes the organization's leaders generated a set of new ways of working. Some of the main ones were:

- General high disclosure (regular information sharing between levels and departments, with very few secrets).

- Easy availability of information about the outside world.

- People being open to exploring new behaviors or policies as conditions change.

- A continuous improvement approach applied to structure and groupings, with easy adjustments when necessary.

- A sense of urgency and high energy, with people being influenced by each other's activities.

To be useful these steps need to precede the typical more technical programming process, not occur as an afterthought. Their main purpose is to provide a context in which to make choices and resolve conflicts among alternatives. If this preplanning work hasn't been done, or if there is no real agreement about the themes and behavioral objectives, then the same battles will occur again and again as the project progresses. The schedule will suffer and the outcome will be a compromise collection of individual victories and losses, rather than a consciously chosen target that relates to the company's desired future.

These up-front steps are not time-wasting frills, but essential elements of an effective project, and they are worth considerable investment of money and attention by key leaders. The investment is returned both in reduced wasted effort later in the project, and in a higher-quality environment that helps the organization better fulfill its mission. The challenge of making the new place opens up a window of opportunity that doesn't occur very often in the history of most organizations—a chance to update ways of working and create a workplace that reinforces them. If leaders don't seize the opportunity early, the window closes and they recreate their old setting in a new location, often at considerable expense and aggravation.

The Programming Process

Following the Phase Zero steps is the programming phase, a relatively comprehensive process of data collection and summary analysis that generates the requirements the workplace design will meet. Data are collected from various groups and levels of the system to define specifically what the setting should accommodate and accomplish, both at the time the project is completed and at some reasonable point in the future, typically five to ten years. The content usually includes areas such as:

Numbers of people to be accommodated

Their basic requirements for space

Types of activities that should be accommodated

Technology requirements

Expected growth and change (rates and patterns)

Communication and interaction patterns

Adjacency requirements (which groups near whom)

Common shared services and where they should be located

This analysis is best performed by experienced professionals, who may be either in-house specialists or hired from outside to do the programming. The outcome is a set of design requirements that can serve as the basis for conceptual and detailed design, when combined with the concepts generated in the Phase Zero work. We won't go into more detailed design steps here, since it would take us beyond the scope and intent of this discussion. The important point to keep in mind for both programming and design is to collect information directly from the users of the workplace, as well as drawing on internal and outside experts.

Employee Involvement in Workplace Decision Processes

As we noted in Chapter Three, the physical setting of work acts as a form of paralanguage, part of a communication system in which the explicit messages may be less important than the implicit, or symbolic, ones. The same thing can be said for the process of planning facilities, especially when the process is explicitly linked to corporate values and philosophies that are intended to promote empowerment, or in its older semantic guise, employee involvement.

The concept, of course, is to empower employees by giving them responsibility and authority to make meaningful decisions about a variety of aspects of their work. This can range from empowering an airline agent to make her own decision about how to resolve an angry customer's problem (without needing approval from a supervisor), to involving staff in decisions about the planning and design of the workplace itself. Many studies have demonstrated that involving employees in the decision process generates both better solutions and more commitment to carrying them out. The surprise for many managers is that involving employees does not necessarily extend, and may even shorten, the overall project process (because decisions are not as likely to be revisited, causing expensive change orders and redesign). There has to be real influence, though, not just going through the motions.

A good example comes from our work with an organization that was implementing the nonterritorial office concept for its sales representatives. Staff suspected that management was using it simply as a way to save money, by squeezing people into less space. Realizing this, the project team wanted to involve the staff in a way that would reassure them that their concerns would be considered. Yet the project was launched in a way that guaranteed failure.

A sales rep council was convened to act as an employee review committee throughout the life of the project. One of their first activities was to review a user needs analysis survey drafted by the project leaders. The council's response was immediate and unequivocal: as far as they were concerned, the survey showed no understanding of how the salespeople worked. It was totally unacceptable to them.

The team leaders said they understood and agreed with the negative feedback. They also said that, unfortunately, it was really too late to change the survey, so they would go ahead with the original version. At this point the sales reps said, in effect, "Listen, don't ask for our opinion, or our public and private endorsement of this process with the other people in the sales group, if you aren't going to listen to what we have to say." Without their support, there was little likelihood the other sales reps would endorse the new way of working.

At this juncture—to the team's credit—the project leaders chose to turn full circle. They began working with the sales reps to completely redo the survey. At the rollout meeting in which the project was launched not long afterward, the sales reps from the employee council enthusiastically supported the planning process. The original survey was never even shown. The commitment to revising the survey was cited as an example of how dedicated the project team was to working with the review committee to identify what the sales force really needed to work productively.

The project leaders' willingness to alter the original schedule was the first step in the development of trust and confidence in the process. It also produced a better survey, which generated more accurate information that could lead them to more effective solutions. In addition, participating in a problem-solving activity in which their ideas were listened to strengthened the sales reps' resolve to exercise their influence for the sake of productivity, not power.

Communication

As a project progresses it is extremely important to keep members of the organization informed about what is happening, where the process is leading, what stage it has reached, and which designs are being created and tested. This can be through many media: newsletters, video broadcasts and tapes, information centers, mockups of proposed work areas, and so on. The greater the variety of modes of communication, the higher the impact is likely to be.

The ongoing communication serves several purposes:

- It helps people know when to raise questions that would otherwise get lost in the shuffle.

- It gives people a chance to test layouts and provide feedback for adjustments.

- It provides involvement in the process and understanding of the intent.

In short, a regular communications effort should be a component of the project, and time and attention should be put into structuring it well. The goal is to keep an informed, enlightened and interested workforce involved in the process of creating or changing their workplace.

Pilot Projects: Changing Incrementally

In talking with people of every sort, we are always surprised by the common belief that just about everyone resists change. The reason we find this curious is that almost everyone we know eagerly embraces all kinds of change in their private lives. The mass exodus of people to beaches on the weekend, to Disneyland, to visit friends and relatives, to tour the Grand Canyon—all of these activities are about seeking change, and not just the short-term change associated with holidays. Most of us also look forward to moving to a better or bigger house, getting a more challenging job, to getting married, having children.

The point, of course, is that we don't resist all changes. We resist changes that undermine our social position, that threaten our sense of competence, that challenge our professional and personal identity, that weaken valued friendships. Propose a change that strengthens these facets of our life and we'll embrace it with gusto. The trick is helping people sense the positive side of something new before they get a chance to experience it. If all they anticipate are negative consequences, then they will resist change.

In the not-too-distant future, virtual reality simulations may satisfy part of the need to experience the future without really living in it. In the meantime, within the context of organizational change, pilot projects can be thought of as a kind of living simulation, a chance to experience altered states of consciousness associated with new ways of working without having to completely abandon all of the familiar rou-

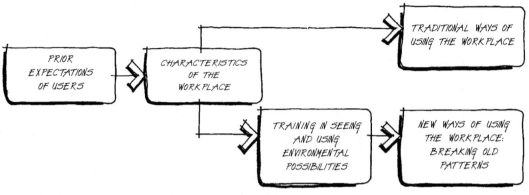

EXPANDING USERS' POSITIVE EXPECTATIONS

tines. As a friend likes to ask, "How do you eat an elephant?" The answer is "One bite at a time."

Pilot projects allow organizations to test new realities in bite-size portions. Pioneers can be groups who already sense the potential benefits. Nonterritorial offices, for example, fundamentally challenge the culture of virtually every organization by eliminating offices assigned to individuals. IBM implemented one of its first pilot projects with a group of systems consultants who volunteered to give up their assigned work stations in exchange for newer technology both in the office and at home. The technology and their own curiosity, as well as management's desire to reduce the amount of space and its associated costs, were the positive factors for trying the change (Becker, Davis, and Sims, 1990).

In another case the incentive was the opportunity to stay in a central city area rather than move to a suburban location more remote from customers and day-to-day services. In the case of the new working group within the Digital Equipment Corporation in Sweden, the incentive for implementing the homey, rather radical form of nonterritorial office was the desire to develop a new way of working that could become a prototype sales demonstration project for a new service business.

Once in place, the experience of the pioneers became the basis for selling other projects within the company. Pilot projects make it possible to demonstrate organizational benefits that otherwise would remain abstract, and in some cases not even imagined. For the nonterritorial offices these benefits included much more teamwork, better informal communication, higher efficiency and effectiveness, and significant cost

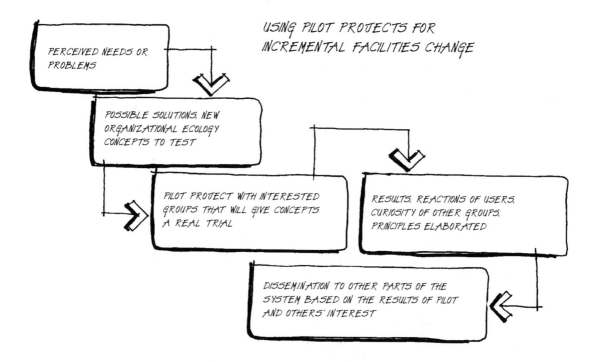

USING PILOT PROJECTS FOR INCREMENTAL FACILITIES CHANGE

PERCEIVED NEEDS OR PROBLEMS

POSSIBLE SOLUTIONS, NEW ORGANIZATIONAL ECOLOGY CONCEPTS TO TEST

PILOT PROJECT WITH INTERESTED GROUPS THAT WILL GIVE CONCEPTS A REAL TRIAL

RESULTS, REACTIONS OF USERS, CURIOSITY OF OTHER GROUPS, PRINCIPLES ELABORATED

DISSEMINATION TO OTHER PARTS OF THE SYSTEM BASED ON THE RESULTS OF PILOT AND OTHERS' INTEREST

savings. A somewhat unanticipated benefit was unprecedented free publicity provided by a horde of journalists constantly searching for something unusual to capture their audience's attention. Pilot projects also tend to lay to rest unwarranted fears about what can't work (when people see that it does, and disaster doesn't strike).

Calling these kinds of pilot projects "experimental" is the kiss of death. Even worse is calling it "research," which is seen as the ultimate academic exercise. Much better to call it, as one of our clients did, an exercise in organizational learning and development. Pretty accurate, actually. Call it whatever works in your organization: prototype services development, market analysis, strategic project initiative, computer-integrated information networking. The goal is to transform abstract concept into concrete experience, and to do it within your own organization where it cannot so easily be dismissed as "something some other crazy company did that has nothing to do with us."

Done well, pilot projects can be a tremendous fulcrum for change. Doing it "well" means taking the time to do the necessary planning, involving all the relevant stakeholders early and meaningfully in the process, considering the social and organizational aspects of the new system as well as its technical and design facets, and learning from things that don't work well and those that do.

The worst that can happen is not to learn anything at all from the project. Sadly, it happens all the time. Problems become viewed as "failures," when they need to be seen as experiences in organizational learning. There are really only two fundamental ways to fail: to make the same mistake repeatedly, or to fear making a mistake so much that the chance of learning from new ways of working is never tried. A bite at a time, pilot projects build confidence through gaining comfort with the new and unknown.

Reviewing and Updating Policies on Workplace Use

If you are going to take the trouble to create a new, more effective workplace, it is necessary to also institute a parallel process to develop policies that support rather than block the rich use of that setting. A variety of groups definitely need to be involved here; they are the ones who can tell you which current policies help them and which get in the way. They can also identify problems or oddities in the way the workplace is used, such as certain very nice seating areas being considered off limits to everyone except officers, who don't know about or want this privilege.

The other data source for updating policies is the model of new ways of working developed in the Phase Zero planning steps. You need to examine how the proposed changes in the workplace will affect the policies, group norms, and management style required to help people use the new setting as intended. Without this step people tend to adapt new places to fit their old ways of working.

Some examples of the areas in which policies might need to be changed include:

- How meeting spaces are scheduled

- Who can use common facilities and equipment

- Processes for changing work station configurations, layouts, and so on

- How much people can personalize their own spots

- Hours of access to the building or specific areas within it

- Security requirements, exclusionary areas, and the like

- Use of offices when their owners are away

The pattern of rules or norms about these and other areas will have a large cumulative impact on whether the potential created by a good workplace concept and design will be realized in practice.

Capitalizing on Positive Attitudes

The work we have been doing on organizational ecology has tended to focus on two complementary areas: the design of workplaces, and the social systems (formal and informal) that influence how people use these workplaces. Focusing too much on these factors can sometimes obscure the third element that influences the impact of the setting: what the individual person brings to it.

We have worked in some instances at developing employees' "environmental competence" to use their workplaces well, but we have paid less attention to another key element that people bring with them to their job: their basic attitude about the workplace and how they should relate to it.

Let us set the scene for this issue by appearing to digress for a moment. Several years ago one of us was in a traffic accident outside Geneva, Switzerland and ended up spending ten days in a hospital overlooking the lake and the mountains (including Mt. Blanc in the distance). It wasn't our finest hour physically, but it turned out to have one big benefit: watching that beautiful scene change over the course of the day. Of course it helped to be in a hospital room that had one of the world's great views. But a lot of the experience had to do with an attitude toward the place, and consequently with decisions made about how to use it.

One conscious decision was to *pay attention* to the changing light each afternoon, to treat looking at the changing scene as a real activity and not to try to do three other things at the same time, as we are so often inclined to do. The other key choice was not to turn on the lights in the room. All other patients would call for their lights as soon as the light outside began to fade, thereby maintaining a constant level of brightness in their rooms. In the process they totally obscured what was happening to the light outside. The nurses thought it was slightly crazy to make a point of not turning the lights on, but we finally got across to them that the best service would be to leave them off.

All of this is a roundabout way of coming to some thoughts about the work environments we have been trying to help shape for clients. One thing we are struck by is the *sense of resignation* that so many people have about their work settings. They seem to accept the fate of working in places that are, at best, not awful. By no means do they expect that the workplace should be stimulating, fun, and a joy to be in.

When we conduct groups focused on environmental preferences, the emphasis is mostly on getting rid of noxious elements and other dissatisfactions. We feel that one of our challenges now is to stimulate a higher level of aspiration about what is possible in workplaces, so that they become positive contributions to the quality of the working experience, not simply less of an irritant.

We have found attitudes so important that we try to run early educational workshops in organizational ecology concepts and examples to get employees thinking in broader terms about their workplaces and what they could be. This helps throughout the project: in framing goals, collecting data, identifying possible pilot projects, and establishing new norms and policies about space use.

We have tended to think of users who pay no attention to the setting, or who do things that neutralize its features (like turning on the lights too soon), as a social system problem where the company's organizational climate constrains what people can do. But after thinking more about the hospital example, it became clear that it is also an individual problem. At least part of the underutilization of a rich setting is caused by our sense of resignation, which leads us to discount possibilities and to feel that high-quality experiences are either irrelevant to work or in active conflict with serious business purposes. Yet the ultimate test for whether people are working hard and well should be what they do, not how they look and where they do it.

Post-Occupancy Tracking

An effective workplace project does not end with users moving into the new space; at that point, the payoff is just beginning. To realize real gains from designing from an organizational ecology point of view, the approach needs to be continued over time. One of the most effective ways to gauge the impact of the setting is to collect baseline data before moving day on productivity, contact patterns, satisfaction, communication, and other areas relating to the goals for the project (especially with respect to new behaviors in ways of working differently).

There should then be a relatively systematic post-occupancy evaluation (POE) using the same dimensions at some specified time after move-in (four to eight months allows time for people to settle in). This can be used to describe effects of the design as well as to identify aspects of the workplace that need further adjustment or redesign. No project is perfect, and collecting early feedback that is actually used sends a message to the employees that the place was made for them and the test of its success is tied to their experiences, not just to theoretical goals.

In general, it helps to institute an ongoing periodic check on how the place is meeting users' needs, how those needs are changing, and whether further big changes will soon be needed in the setting. This can be done with a fairly low-key process of observations and occasional focus groups. The idea is to make regular assessment a natural process, not something that is done only when a groundswell of dissatisfaction appears to be building into a crisis.

CHAPTER ELEVEN

The Role of Leadership: Championing the Workplace Vision

Having discussed a variety of activities and issues related to planning effective and innovative workplaces, we need to turn to considerations of who can make this happen. Since many of the working assumptions we have been using vary considerably from the typical "business as usual" culture, their success depends to a great degree on the ability and willingness of key leaders to point the way by shaping and consistently supporting the change process.

Some people, regardless of their formal title or position, are natural influence leaders with a personal interest in organizational ecology. Members of the organization look to them for ideas, inspiration, and support when it comes to thinking about how the workplace can be created, or managed, to help the organization prosper. What characterizes such natural leaders is a clear sense of what they are trying to accomplish using facility planning, design, and management as tools, and the readiness to use resources in imaginative ways to invent solutions that solve the organization's real problems.

We have seen these people at the top of organizations, where formal position and informal influence mesh. Pekka Roine, who was the country area manager for Digital Equipment Corporation in Finland, is this kind of person. He was known throughout the company as full of ideas that initially seemed to be wild but often turned out to make sense. Eliminating closed offices, introducing cellular and cordless telephones, removing all status indications, and providing swing sets and patio furniture for meetings challenged conventional expectations about what the office should be.

Natural influence leaders can also be people like Alan Drake, the facilities manager at Hexcel Corporation, headquartered in Pleasanton, California. For him the important characteristics were not position, but an understanding of organizational ecology and the ability to articulate a vision of how the facilities might contribute to improved organizational performance, combined with the credibility to convince senior management to support a new initiative more or less on faith. Drake was able to transform what had been conceptualized as a straightforward real estate deal to reduce occupancy costs into a project directly addressing fundamental organizational challenges, such as the way senior management related to staff and the desire to reduce boundaries and barriers among different operating divisions.

A second kind of organizational leader is the senior management person whose position within the organization holds special responsibilities. These managers, in particular, are the focus of this chapter. They are often officers of the company at the level of director, vice president, or higher. Although they may control space decisions, typically neither their training nor corporate experiences have prepared them to view workplace issues as falling within their own domain. Yet because members of an organization look to its leaders for guidance about what they should pay attention to and how they should spend their time and energy, leaders play a critical organizational ecology role: to send the message that how the workplace is planned, designed, and managed has important consequences for how the organization functions.

To play this kind of leadership role, at the very minimum leaders need to understand enough about organizational ecology to articulate a vision of how the workplace can become a tool for productive work. This vision can take many forms. We once worked with a giant manufacturing firm that was trying to figure out how to use its main manufacturing site to best advantage. Over time, as the company had grown, some functions and groups had ended up in leased space off site, or in more or less random locations within the main site. Everyone agreed that something should be done to rationalize the location of the troops. Should everyone come back to the main site? If some groups should be off site, were the right ones currently there? And where should those groups at the main site be located in relation to each other?

These are fundamental organizational questions. The answers affect cross-division and departmental communication patterns that can undermine the product development process, service delivery, and sales efforts that cross divisional lines. Unfortunately, there are no single simple answers to these questions. But there is a lot of information that could be brought to bear in an intelligent fashion to inform the discussion. The kind of analysis that would have been helpful would have focused on desired future work patterns first, and then on their underlying assumptions, and the evidence supporting them, concerning the distances at which "proximity" actually contributed to informal interaction. Would co-locating groups on the same site but half a mile apart significantly improve the nature of serendipitous informal contact and communication?

Unfortunately, no key leaders were centrally involved in the discussion of the organization's ecology issues. The problem had been delegated to the facilities people and that was the end of it as far as the executives were concerned. In a sense the process was doomed from the start to have relatively little impact.

In this chapter we will discuss a variety of important roles that need to be played when leaders shape the ecology of their organizations. It is a fairly long list of possible roles and is meant to be suggestive rather than exhaustive. Each situation calls for some forethought and understanding about the role that the leader could play before he or she jumps into the content of the problem.

Space standards, for example, which most senior managers do not consider an especially important management issue, often unwittingly influence in powerful ways how the organization functions. Companies such as USWest and Steelcase, who are beginning to experiment with new forms of executive offices, have realized that the costs of space standards that isolate executives on "executive row" floors, and within these floors in palatial offices that further isolate the executives from one another, have minimally to do with the amount of space available and the cost of that space. Far more important is that the space standards are exerting tremendous control over how executives relate to each other on a day-to-day basis, on what information they share, and on what they know

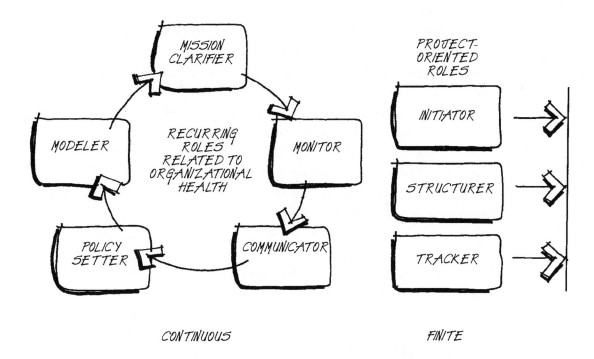

SUCCESSFUL PROJECTS REQUIRE DISTINCTION BETWEEN
CONTINUOUS AND FINITE PROJECT MANAGEMENT ROLES.

about what is happening in other departments or divisions and within
their own staff. To make sure that what seem like trivial or just technical
decisions are considered in terms of their organizational implications,
there are a number of roles organizational leaders can play.

The Many Roles of Leaders

Developing a healthy pattern of organizational ecology doesn't happen
just because it is the thing to do, but because people who can influence
others help to make it happen. There are a number of key roles or activities that must be done by someone who has power in the system. These
include the following.

SETTING DIRECTION

One of the most obvious leader roles is to be active in setting overall
directions for the enterprise. This role needs to be fulfilled in order for
other ecology-related activities to succeed. As we noted in the previous

chapter, the leader needs to be concerned about whether there is an updated, agreed-upon statement about vision, mission, identity, philosophy, and the like. If these are missing, there is no real context in which to embed the choices and directions that a facilities project needs to take. All kinds of choices and conflicts come around again and again throughout a project if these initial directions are not clear.

With respect to creating high-performance workplaces, the critical focus of the leader must be to ensure that the company's values and philosophy are not only articulated, but that those influencing the planning and design and management of the workplace on a daily basis are actively seeking ways of incorporating these values into workplace decisions. It is easy to find organizations today, for example, that talk in their philosophy statements about empowering staff. It is much harder to find examples of corporations that without apparent effort directly involve all staff directly in early planning decisions about the nature of the workplace. Organizations need to pay attention to how the values they articulate are actually reflected in workplace practices.

DEFINING KEY CHALLENGES

A second key role is leading the effort to define the system's key challenges or success factors. What areas of action will be most critical to the success or failure of the enterprise in the next five to ten years? What do we have to make sure that we do very well, because if we don't the organization is not likely to survive?

This role means projecting future demands, constraints, environmental shifts, and information technology trends, and then using this information to identify broad strategy issues that have to be well managed in order to keep ahead of the game. This information must then be made accessible to those charged with creating high-performance workplaces.

Achieving this on-line awareness of organizational directions requires engaging management in detailed discussions about what challenges and opportunities the enterprise is facing, and getting from the discussions a result that does not sound like every other company in the world that wants to have great quality, great service, and minimal costs. Whatever the results of these discussions, they must be used as real guides for making choices about how to allocate time, attention, space, and other resources.

SETTING THE FEEL OF THE WORKPLACE

Just as at a national level a President Reagan or Bush creates a different philosophical climate from a Kennedy or Clinton, the organization's leaders set its climate. Thus another key early role is being a driver for defining the overall desired "feel" of the company's work settings. This should be closely tied to efforts to define a philosophy about the kind of organization and climate the members wish to maintain and be a part of. Again a leader should not be doing this unilaterally, but should be making sure that there is a process for doing it with meaningful results that can be used to guide facilities policies and decisions.

For example, a recent client group of managers decided that they would commit themselves to creating and maintaining a truly first-rate workplace for their employees, so that they would become the "employer of choice" in their geographic region. There followed from this a set of principles concerning the need to provide employees with individual control over temperature, light, and noise, as well as access to support systems, such as day care and quality food, that up to then had not been considered relevant.

Although the discussion occurred in the context of decisions about the workplace, they were really defining the kind of relationship they wanted to maintain between the organization and its members, and the culture they hoped to foster. If these kinds of principles are relatively clear and widely shared and understood, then many facilities projects can rather easily incorporate and strengthen them. Having a strong organizational culture reduces the need for formalized rules and control mechanisms since people faced with a decision are constantly asking themselves, "Is this what we should be doing if we want to empower our employees, or speed decision making, or reduce the importance of status indicators?"

MONITORING

One of the more amorphous roles a leader needs to play is that of a general monitor of the quality of "fit" between an organization and its work settings. This role includes making sure that data exist about how the workplace is performing, how people feel about their experiences in it, and how well the upcoming demands on the system can be met by the current facilities. Some leaders typically flip into this role when something triggers their attention, such as running out of places to put new employees when they are first hired. Rather than being driven by an on-off switch, this role needs continuity in order to be effective. Many workplace changes can be done as a matter of course if they are timely, or they can be major problems, eat up unnecessary time and resources, and cause losses in performance when they occur too late.

One prerequisite for fulfilling this role is curiosity—about people in settings and how those settings are affecting their performance and experiences. Key tasks in this role can of course be delegated to facilities people or to other leaders, but the commitment to continuity needs to be signalled by the behavior of the senior leaders. They have to demonstrate that they want this factor tracked just as they do other business factors such as trends in markets or manufacturing costs.

INITIATING PROJECTS

When there is a recognized need for some sort of workplace change, be it a new facility, a rework of the existing one, or a major change in why and how the current place is used, someone in the organization needs to take a clear role in establishing the start, goals, and boundaries for the project. This includes structuring and signing off on the planning process itself: objectives, time frame, budget guidelines, decision processes, structure of the project team or teams, and criteria for who should be involved in which tasks and phases of the project.

A special role for senior management can be ensuring that more diverse players are brought into the project early on, and that they play a real role in it. These "nontraditional" people may be from within the organization, such as a small group of staff with a particular interest in child care, or someone who has developed considerable experience through earlier projects about a highly technical subject, such as fire safety in computer rooms. Nontraditional specialists may also be from the outside—human factors specialists and organizational ecologists, for instance, or lighting consultants who have greater depth of understanding of some technical or human issues than typical project team members.

One important aspect of this role is not just helping identify the right kind of people, but making sure that they are being used effectively. How these specialists are selected and integrated into the project shapes how the whole project will play itself out. Getting clarity about the intent, structure, and roles for the project early on will save enormous time and energy down the road, which otherwise can be wasted in power struggles or grappling with ambiguous, unproductive tasks.

The limits of the role are just as crucial here as is its content. You must walk a fine line: being involved in the overall structuring of a project without planting yourself so firmly in the middle that people in other project roles are dependent on you or reluctant to act on their own. An important way to think about this role is that it is part engineer, implementing a process, and part facilitator, helping create the conditions within which people can be involved at appropriate points and levels of decision making, so that they feel ownership of the resulting workplace. If they do not, you will always be trying to sell them something that they will not be inclined to buy.

The role should *not* be played as the ultimate source of all taste and wisdom about design decisions. The design criteria should be heavily influenced by the output of the kinds of activities in earlier stages that were described above, so that directions and principles have come out of an inclusionary process, not just the leader's particular preferences or style.

The other key aspect of this role is that of communicator, sharing information with the total organization about the project, its goals, the expected effects on the organization and its members, the time frame, and the different stages. This communication helps set realistic expectations, while also signaling that this effort is considered important by the system's leaders and therefore worthy of people contributing their own time and attention. We have seen many projects where the leadership did not play the communicator role, and members therefore had to be "resold" on participating every time a new activity came up. Their commitment should be obtained in a connected, global manner, not in bits and pieces.

TRACKING AND REVIEW

As a new facility or a renovation project runs its course, the leader needs to stay involved in the role of the overall "client." This does not mean attending all project meetings and approving every detail. It does mean holding periodic reviews, testing developments for their degree of fit with the overall principles, goals, and design criteria, and testing how well people are being kept informed and involved in the process.

The key here is to be able to track the progress without smothering it. There is a real danger of smothering because of the positional power that most top leaders have in their organizations. People will listen, interpret, and defer to the leader's implied wishes, even when they are not intended to be anything more than off-the-cuff expressions of personal opinions. In a bank we were working with, for example, the president mentioned in a casual conversation with architects that he thought open-plan work stations would probably make sense. Without any further testing of this idea, open-plan work stations were treated as a program requirement. It was not until much later in the project, when high-level professional staff members vigorously questioned the merits of work stations, that the issue resurfaced for the president. He wanted to know why work stations were specified in the first place!

On the flip side of this situation are leaders who get involved disproportionately in areas where they are interested but not especially knowledgeable and therefore not the appropriate decision makers. A few years ago we consulted with a multibillion-dollar company where the president was spending his time (and the project's time budget) choosing the color of the brick for various exterior surfaces; at the same time, he was uninvolved and basically uninterested in decisions about the overall space planning concepts and the locations of different groups within the building.

SETTING POLICY

In addition to roles played in major projects, the leader has an ongoing role: the establishment of effective workplace management policies (as we discussed in the previous chapter). This role is somewhat like that of a playwright who helps adapt scripts to the particular medium in which they are being used. The leader's orientation in the policy area should be to help create work conditions that support members in a variety of tasks and styles of work, without assuming that there is one best way for all employees, or even a best way for a given employee at different times and conditions. Policies should be experienced as supportive and helpful, not as mainly constraints that are being enforced for administrative consistency and convenience.

For example, we were involved with a computer company that seemed to be outgrowing its space. We worked with the top management team to define the problem and causes, and as a result of this diagnosis most of our work emphasized the role of key managers as policy setters. They were applying big-company standards to a simple startup operation, resulting in a felt lack of freedom among the staff and an underutilization of their premises. As one staff member put it, it was a $10,000 organization wearing a $100,000,000 culture.

By focusing on their role as policy makers, the organization's leaders were able to define some less constraining rules. The key one was to free up procedures so that people would be encouraged to be creative about how and where they did their work. This effort had an investment cost in terms of our time and the executives' time, but almost no out-of-pocket facility costs since the new ways of working enabled the firm to avoid taking on another expensive lease at a time when they needed their cash for growing the business.

Policies governing how the workplace is used and managed will have the greatest cumulative impact over the long haul. The effects are there day in and day out, overlaid on where and how people do their work. One way to think of this role of policy setter is that it is like a snowplow, clearing the streets so that the users can do what they need to do without anything getting in their way.

Of course, leaders don't usually say to themselves, "Let's develop some policies that will really hamstring these folks." But this is the net effect of a lot of the unexamined choices that are made because they've always been made that way. Something as seemingly simple as the requirement that no changes be made to a work station without following a predetermined change order process is a good example. When a desk is facing the wrong way, or an additional storage unit is needed, a tedious process that can take days if not weeks is often initiated, all the while making it difficult for the employee to work efficiently. It would be much simpler, faster, and more effective to empower janitorial staff, for example, to respond directly and on the spot to requests for help to reposition furniture within an office or work station, as long as the move does not pose any safety problems.

This raises the question of another nondesign factor that affects the use of workplaces: the social climate. Besides formal policies, groups develop informal rules of the game about how people should look, what they can do in different spaces, and the like. Who enforces these rules can sometimes be amusing. We once worked in a firm where at set times a woman appeared on the floor pushing a break cart laden with coffee, soft drinks, chocolate chip cookies, and other snacks. When she arrived she rang a bell, and like Pavlov's dogs all of us dropped whatever we were doing and rushed out to meet the cart. One day we did this after we had been in a meeting for hours, during which time all of us, including several senior managers, had loosened our ties and unbuttoned our shirts. Immediately on seeing us the cart lady said, "Gentlemen, your ties" and in an instant all our hands were at our necks buttoning our shirts and straightening our ties. Only afterward did we realize that the cart lady was the person setting the standards for professional comportment!

In relation to the workplace, we have seen facility managers prohibit managers and professionals from positioning their desks so that they could sit perpendicular to the door because it looked "unprofessional." These kind of informal social norms can undermine new directions in which the organization wants to move.

The leader's role as policy setter can, and in cases like those just mentioned should, expand into one that includes influencing group norms as well formal policies. This is an important area for the leader to be aware of, but it is harder to influence than written policies, since it is by definition informal and formed by group consensus rather than managerial pronouncements. The role here is probably best played as one of leading by example, modeling the desired behaviors and encouraging them when they are observed, as noted below, but it can also include leading an examination of group norms and their effects on workplace utilization. This legitimizes it as an area for conscious diagnosis and problem solving rather than being left as a set of untested assumptions. The ultimate goal in this area is to make sure the policies and norms are consistent with the mission and goals of the enterprise.

MODELING

This role is different from the others mentioned, in that it does not focus on organizational ecology itself. It simply means using the day-to-day work tasks as opportunities to demonstrate the possibilities that exist in the setting. In short, leaders should pay attention to their own work processes. An example would be getting out and using a variety of settings and resources in the workplace, not staying hunkered down in your own office or work station all day as a model of efficient "rootedness."

As a case in point, the SAS headquarters building in Stockholm includes an interior "street" with an outdoor café area. Several of the company's executives often meet with people in the café rather than in their private offices. This accomplishes two things. It sets a different tone for the interchange (they are conversations rather than meetings), and it sets an example of exploiting the potential of the building to support diverse ways of working.

This is much better than the opposite pattern where an interesting and experimental new setting gets created, and then the leaders of the organization continue to use space the way they did in the old setting. At the least, this is an ambiguous message: "Our new concepts are good for you, but they have nothing to do with me." It is more usually taken as a stronger message: that nothing has really changed except the walls and furniture. So people fall right back into the safety of their old patterns of doing tasks where and how they've always been done. It is not enough to make good spots for working in alternative ways and then just hope for the best. If you really want them to be used, you will generally have to prime the pump by consciously using them yourself, and getting other leaders of the organization to do likewise.

This kind of behavior puts everyone on notice that it is perfectly legitimate to conduct serious business meetings in comfortable, informal surroundings. The objective of the modeling role is to use yourself as an example of the variety of ways the total workplace can be used as a setting. It may require, in addition, sending explicit messages to that effect. If you are indirect and too subtle, people may interpret your behavior as reflecting your privilege to work anywhere you choose, and not see it as having anything to do with themselves.

We should also mention that a side benefit of leaders getting around is that they naturally become more aware of what's happening in the system. It is an extension of the notion of management by walking around, which tended to assume that you were either wandering about or you were in your office doing "real work." It is much easier for organizational leaders to stay in touch with the organization by doing "real work" in lots of different places at different times; and encouraging others to do likewise enhances the sense of connectedness for the system as a whole.

Preparation for Roles

We are aware of the fact that we have been describing a wide-ranging set of roles for an organization's leaders to play in matters of organizational ecology, on top of all the other aspects of running the business. Just talking about them is not enough to equip people to play these roles. Some will do them better than others, and everyone will play some of the roles better than other roles. There are, however, some actions that can improve your abilities to fulfill these roles as a part of your overall leadership of the enterprise.

TRAINING SESSIONS AND WORKSHOPS

There are seminars and programs that you could attend to learn more about design, planning, organizational culture, and their impact on the performance of the enterprise. Just as with other areas of management, every experience of this type tends to open up new possibilities if the person takes them seriously. The field of organizational ecology has an emerging body of knowledge about the nature of work settings, their impact on users, and theories and concepts to guide choices in shaping places. The better informed leaders are about these matters, the more likely they are to be able to do the kinds of things we have been describing above, as well as help others to play such roles.

We have often begun our own work with a new client system by conducting what we call a physical settings workshop. This is a general review of concepts and examples from organizational ecology, including what people are doing on the cutting edge. Included in this is a beginning diagnosis of the particular style and needs of the organization, along with participants' feelings about areas where new concepts might fit their needs.

We work hard to keep the session focused on ideas and possibilities, rather than having it turn into a designing session where choices or decisions must be made. There is a tendency in American business to want to have decisions and actions come out of every event, so we try to keep the focus on the goal of expanding the shared "image bank" and not on reaching consensus or making a decision. We feel this is needed to form a common frame of reference for whatever the leaders do afterward, so that they are working from a common knowledge set.

EXPLORATION AND SCOUTING

Even with a base of knowledge about workplace ecology, it is hard to keep current on what is being done in this area. It can be extremely helpful to get out on field trips and see what other organizations have been doing. You obviously can't do this sort of thing full time (unless that's your chosen role), but the occasional visit can be worth months of talking about possibilities. There is tremendous value in actually seeing something in place and being used.

To get the most out of such visits, you have to look at what is there, of course—really seeing the setting and its possibilities. But in addition it is important to talk about how it got that way: the concepts that were used, the choices made, the intentions behind them, the process used, who was involved in it, and so on. The value of a visit is in the total story, not just in the look of the physical end product. It's also useful to have along someone knowledgeable about the workplace and organizational ecology who can help explain and interpret what you are seeing.

ROLE NEGOTIATION

One of the key factors that make any organizational role succeed is the degree of clarity of expectations about the role. The person playing the role should understand its requirements, and those with whom they work should have the same set of expectations.

The implication for leaders' roles in organizational ecology is fairly obvious: when playing one or more of the above roles, leaders should use some sort of role clarification or role negotiation process, rather than keeping their intentions in their heads and hoping that others respond appropriately. Getting clear about what the leader's roles will and won't be can help free others to do their own parts. It also reduces the number of mismatches in expectations during the process, so that different parties see and interpret events in the same way.

When a major project is initiated, this sort of role clarification should occur early, since it influences all other aspects of the process. Even if there is no major project per se, it helps to periodically have a discussion about the various ongoing roles that affect the shape and use of the workplace. Tracking workplace performance and knowing when to take action are much harder if it's not clear who is tracking or monitoring what or who can legitimately raise issues for consideration by management.

USE OF APPROPRIATE SUPPORTING RESOURCES

One of the smartest things that leaders can do is understand their own limitations. Knowing what not to expect from yourself is as important as having high expectations for your knowledge. Even though we have been describing quite a few different areas where we feel a leader needs to play a key role, those areas are not intended to block or downplay the necessity for contributions from others. Leaders need to be well informed about the varieties of professional expertise that are available in this area, including facilities design, master planning, facilities management, information systems, and organization development. Just as in medicine, we need to know what specialized expertise is needed and be willing to trust detailed analyses and decisions by such professionals.

Some organizations have these specialists residing in house, while others hire them as consultants when needed. Even the facility management function, which has traditionally been an internal, dedicated group, is more and more frequently being outsourced to contractors. The mix of in-house versus on-call resources is obviously a judgment that has to be made based on the system's needs and resources, and how they are likely to change over time.

Leaders probably need to have at least some professionals in house who understand how the ecology of the organization—its decisions about location, about space allocation, and about policies governing use of the setting—affect individual, group, and ultimately organizational performance. Such professionals serve as an available sounding board for ideas and concerns in the workplace area. They also help leaders shape the overall pattern of inside and outside resources.

The other function that knowledgeable people can play in house is to provide feedback to the leaders about how well they are playing the roles described in this chapter. Leaders need to get such feedback in a timely and accurate manner in order to avoid drifting along without any course corrections.

INTEREST AND CURIOSITY

Finally, it seems to us that people are more likely to play an effective leadership role in the area of workplace design and management if they are in fact interested in the area and curious about learning more. For some leaders this is a natural affinity; for others it may need to be cultivated. We don't expect everyone to share our interests and enthusiasm, but there does seem to be a general need for basic curiosity about places and how they affect people in order to be an effective leader about workplace ecology processes and issues. Seeking out information and getting involved in educational activities can help kindle that interest, as can simply dealing more directly with the issues in workplace design.

If leaders feel after giving it a shot that they still have little or no interest in being involved in the ecology of their organization, they will probably not be very effective in the roles described in this chapter. It may be better to link up with another key leader and support them in playing such roles, so that there is a partnership leading the effort.

Keeping Roles in Focus

Effective workplace management requires one or more committed top leaders who are willing to play a number of key roles that influence the ecology of the organization, from examining basic direction and values through influencing and monitoring space use over time. The leaders need to be clear about the roles, negotiate that clarity with others in the system, and be willing to set boundaries so that they do not get overinvolved in ways that block others' contributions.

As a way of summarizing, we will briefly review the leadership roles in relation to the organizational ecology planning activities discussed in the previous chapter.

1. *Overall direction.* First, there are three key activities that need to be done as a part of general direction of the enterprise, whether applied to organizational ecology or not:

- Keeping the vision, values, and mission of the organization in focus, and periodically reviewing them to gain updated agreement among the members.

- Identifying change directions for organizational goals, size, strategy, technology, culture, and the like; making sure that they are visible and understood.

- Setting overall standards for assessing the system's organizational health: criteria to be used, how they will be measured, and so on (such as the model described in Chapter Two).

2. *Workplace impact.* Second, there are certain other roles, more specifically related to organizational ecology, that are aimed at generating and using good current information about the impact of the organization's work settings and facilities management process. These include:

- Structuring regular periodic data collection on the effects of workplace designs and use policies, including problem areas to be tackled.

- Being observant about the impact of workplaces on everyone in the organization, including yourself. This requires moving about to become more aware of the variety of settings and for the overall "feel" of the place as a whole.

3. *Decisions about facilities.* Third are roles related to the process of structuring how facilities decisions are handled:

- Structuring a workplace management function of some sort to ensure that it is efficient, effective, creative, responsive to users' needs, and supported by the organization's leaders.

- Structuring facilities decision processes, including defining different types of decisions, who should be involved in them, and how much.

- Establishing a process and standards for integrating the organization's work settings into the surrounding environment and community in positive ways.

4. *Leadership by example.* Finally, there is an important role that stems from simply being a highly visible and influential member of the organization:

- Modeling (in one's own work style) an awareness of place and a willingness to experiment in how work settings are used day to day.

5. *Senior managers.* Dropping down to the positions or levels below the CEO or the executive committee, there are a number of important organizational ecology leadership roles that should be played by senior executives or managers, mirroring some of those for the CEO:

- Actively observing and thinking about the impact of workplaces on themselves and others in the organization.

- Agreeing to and actively disseminating overall mission, values, philosophy, and the like.

- Discussing and supporting long-term place strategies.

- Helping to shape overall facilities decision processes.

- Actively participating in workplace decisions for their level.

- Supporting their own suborganizations in consciously shaping their work environments.

- Modeling effective environmental behavior in their own ways of working.

Leadership roles need to be defined so that they do not freeze out effective participation by others in the system, who should also be encouraged to influence the workplaces that influence their own effectiveness. By describing these behaviors as leading, we do not mean to imply that they are out of bounds to people who are not executives.

High-performing organizations need high-performing facilities that easily accommodate unpredictable changes in organizational size and structure, that support teamwork, and that motivate and energize staff and management alike. Getting there takes managers who believe that the way space is allocated and configured is much more than simply a cost issue or a matter of corporate image. These facility decisions affect the thousands of daily work and communication experiences that ultimately determine how well business gets done. Getting them right is a fundamental component of management strategy.

CHAPTER TWELVE

Quality and Return on Investment: Spending Money Where It Will Make a Difference

What's the best car? The answer is, "It depends." A Porsche is great for speed, but a terrible choice for hauling hay. A station wagon would be awful in a road race, and any new car is a poor choice in the free-for-all of Boston traffic. When we think of quality criteria for cars, whether it be cost, reliability, durability, speed, beauty, carrying capacity, resale value, safety, or novelty, we are essentially defining what's good in terms of fit with the intended purposes. The concept of fit forces us to define "best" in terms of what is most appropriate for the situation: function, use patterns, expected length of ownership, nature of person driving, range of environmental conditions, and so on. The right car for a five-mile commute during the day along city streets in a temperate climate is unlikely to be the same car preferred for a hundred-mile daily commute across the Minnesota prairie.

Ironically, we often think more about the criteria we should employ for selecting the family car than we do about the criteria for selecting our organization's workplace strategies, even though these constitute the organization's most expensive resource, after salaries and wages. Yet the principles of fit that we apply almost without thinking to car purchases are just as useful in thinking about the kind of facilities that are needed to help the organization move forward.

Headquarters buildings are discernibly different in form, materials, and furnishings from back-office buildings; executive suites bear little resemblance to secretarial work stations. It is not difficult deciding into which overall category a building falls. It can be much harder deciding what is the right level of quality (and what are the valid criteria) for a building within a given category.

Relative Definitions of Workplace Quality

Many U.S. organizations are beginning to question their own long-standing definition of quality. The Eastman Kodak Company, based in Rochester, New York, is an example. Kodak has always prided itself on building only "quality" facilities. It still does. But in the face of new competitive pressures, the definition of quality has shifted from building for the millennium to building for an expected occupancy period. In fitting out leased space, for instance, carpets are now bought to last three to five years, not twenty, because Kodak often vacates leased space in the shorter time frame (Becker, Davis, and Sims, 1990). Why pay for quality that will never be used?

One trend in corporate real estate management is to consider building form and building systems in terms of their residual value. How easily and for how much money could a building be leased or sold in the future if Kodak's business plans changed and the company wanted to vacate the building and install new tenants? Other major organizations such as Digital Equipment Corporation and IBM are asking similar questions, and in the process redefining their concept of quality. At the heart of the reevaluation of what constitutes quality is a concern for having a clearer strategy about the purposes of buildings in use over time.

This way of looking at quality may mean spending more money rather than less in some areas, but with a clear idea about why the higher quality fits with both business plans and market realities. For example, when constructing a building, Digital Equipment Corporation now considers spending more money than it used to for support systems (such as advanced communications technology) that will give the building flexibility over time, thereby allowing it to be used in a variety of unspecified ways by either the company's own groups or by other tenants or owners. IBM has a program to enhance the quality of undeveloped sites through landscaping and site development so that both the value of the sites and their marketability are enhanced whether IBM decides to sell them or use them for its own purposes (Becker, Davis, and Sims, 1990).

In both of these examples the amount of money invested is considered in terms of the return on investment. Unless there are compelling user needs, it makes no sense to install building management systems that price a building outside the range its particular market can bear. The operating principle is the same one most of us use in thinking about renovations or improvements in our own homes: except for some special need, it is counterproductive to spend a great deal more on an improvement than you are likely to be able to recoup when you sell the house. A key factor in this assessment, of course, is the expected duration of use. A change that makes sense if you can realistically plan on living in the house for twenty years will be entirely different from what makes sense if you believe you may be moving within two years.

There is no single answer, then, to what constitutes "quality," but there can be a single objective: to provide the best possible support for the full range of activities critical to organizational survival, at the lowest possible cost, over an expected period of use.

Defining quality in terms of fit has additional implications. For one, it suggests the need to rethink what constitute luxuries, frills, and sound business requirements. Some of the things that have been conventionally treated as functional requirements in a headquarters building, such as expensive materials and distinctive designs demonstrating executive status, may from this perspective be seen as unnecessary frills. Materials and finishes undoubtedly are one manifestation of "quality," but if the focus is on allocating scarce resources to meet business objectives, then the definition of quality might well shift. A "quality" building would then be one that most strongly supports, through its design, how the organization is intended to function.

In the DEC Finland headquarters in Helsinki this took the form of providing a sauna and swimming pool on the top floor. DEC's U.S.–based corporate real estate group was initially appalled by what seemed like an outrageous luxury. After some discussions they came to understand that in the context of doing business in Finland this was simply a fundamental business tool. It is in the sauna that many critical business meetings are closed. It is difficult to be angry or combative when sitting naked in a dimly lit, 100-degree room.

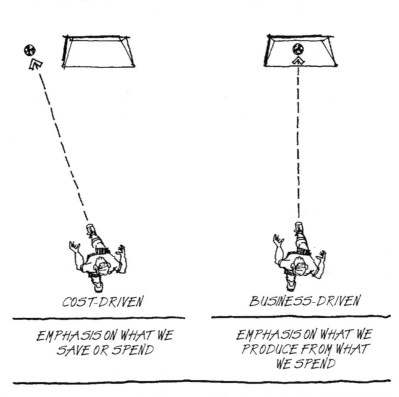

COST-DRIVEN

BUSINESS-DRIVEN

EMPHASIS ON WHAT WE
SAVE OR SPEND

EMPHASIS ON WHAT WE
PRODUCE FROM WHAT
WE SPEND

IN A BUSINESS-DRIVEN WORKPLACE, THE GOAL IS TO BECOME
MORE COMPETITIVE, NOT JUST REDUCE COSTS.

In other instances spending money on business objectives may mean providing highly pleasant informal meeting areas, or cellular telephones and portable faxes, or a building whose form and interior layout increase the probability of a range of face-to-face communication opportunities. It can mean providing amenities in back offices, from fitness facilities to pleasant cafeterias and break areas; these amenities have traditionally been more closely associated with head offices, but they can help attract and retain highly desirable staff. It could in some cases mean reducing the headquarters facilities to the bare minimum, making them comfortable but lean, so that resources can be devoted to better-quality facilities in field locations.

New Isn't Always Better

In thinking about quality, people usually assume that something new is always better, but it isn't always the case. Fashion designer Ralph Lauren has turned this insight into a steady stream of profits. He understands that people will pay top prices for new goods that appear and feel like they are old. From faded jeans to stonewashed shirts, people have voted with their checkbooks and credit cards for clothes that are instantaneously comfortable, that fit as though they have been worn for years. In fact, there are certain aspects of newness—and oldness—that we like, and some that we don't. The key is understanding which are important, which are nice but not necessary, which are valuable as a change, and which may be useless or even counterproductive.

A worthy goal—and it is possible—is to capture the best of the new in a way that preserves the best of the old. One of our colleagues in Société Générale, a large French bank, recently redeveloped an office block called the Trocadero, located in one of the most fashionable districts in Paris. The developers kept or rebuilt all the visible features of the old nineteenth-century building: fluted columns, wonderful woodwork, tall windows, superb craftsmanship. Behind all that they installed the latest in heating and air conditioning, wiring, and plumbing technology. The result is an office development that commands the highest rents in Paris, and a magnificent, historically based structure that functions perfectly in today's high-technology world.

Functionality, technology, aesthetics, and history all count in the total workplace experience. This is not a big revelation, but it's hard to think of many organizations we have visited where leaders have understood that a "quality" work environment is not just ergonomic seating and good task lighting, not just individual temperature and ventilation controls, and not (most certainly) just new furniture and a flashy design. The fact is that workplaces that have none of these features, but that are comfortable in the sense of taking a human imprint, of being what we called in an earlier book "people-places" rather than "object-places," are most likely to provide high-quality experiences for their users. We tend to associate these kinds of environments with certain kinds of professionals, such as computer programmers and advertising copy writers. But what evidence is there that accountants, finance managers, or human resource staff appreciate and are motivated by dull, impersonal surroundings?

Distinctive Character

The hallmark of a workplace that fits is that you know you have arrived at someplace distinctive, even though it may be recognizable as a standard type or even part of an overall corporate identity. And the distinctiveness generally comes from how people are using the place, as much as from what is *in* it. This sense of place does not have to be associated with or "owned" by a single person. Work groups of from twenty-five to fifty people can collectively make decisions about the type of furniture to have and how to arrange it and in the process can strengthen their own group identity.

Spending effort on better use of existing facilities can result in better value for money than spending more money on creating new designs. New designs—furniture, finishes, carpeting, lighting—by themselves are unlikely to create a better, more effective work environment. If only it were that easy.

We've done several studies in which new office designs costing millions of dollars were basically a wash compared with the old office environment they replaced: staff satisfaction level remained the same. Employees appreciated the cleanliness and greater physical comfort of new furniture, and hated the new rules that prevented them from eating at their desk, or rearranging furniture, or hanging posters on walls, or tacking up paper on panes, or bringing in their own task lights.

The case of Lloyds of London is a good illustration (Becker, 1988). One year after their new head office building (one of the most expensive ever built in Europe at the time) was occupied, the building manager estimated that $50 million in renovations were needed, ranging from more lifts and cable capacity to new wall and ceiling finishes and surfaces. These design dysfunctions directly affected the nature of the business process, since almost all of the activity in this insurance marketplace depends on direct, face-to-face contacts. Slow elevators and meeting areas that occupants found unpleasant undermined in a myriad of small ways the fragile social processes that were the foundation of all business activity. Although the building's construction system is unique, these processes did not receive sufficient attention in the original design program.

The issue is not about spending money versus not spending it. It is spending whatever funds are available in a way that reaps their maximum potential. And that means spending the time and effort to find out what employees really care about, not assuming that management knows what they should care about. It means working to understand what aspects of the old situation should be preserved and which ones should be relegated to the dustbin.

It especially means understanding the system's fundamental business objectives. This has nothing to do, per se, with design image, but everything to do with work effectiveness. One of our facility manager friends found, after spending hundreds of thousands of dollars on new systems furniture, that the employees' attitude was "ho-hum." He then gave all employees $100 to buy any kind of office accessory they wanted (a total cost of $10,000, a drop in the bucket compared to the total project budget). He had never in his professional life seen a group of employees so excited, enthusiastic, and committed to the organization. He was particularly amazed (and pleased) that it was achieved with no inflation of the budget. The distinctiveness of the resulting place was achieved by simply allowing the diversity of the users to be expressed.

The Nature of Resources

To do an effective job of allocating resources in shaping the ecology of the organization, it helps to have a clear understanding of what these resources are. One class of resources is scarce, finite, and nonrenewable, like using up coal. Using them for workplace planning and construction represents a tradeoff decision. Money is the obvious example: costs of buildings, furniture, equipment, and the like; costs for designers and consultants in the planning process; costs of staff to work on the project; and costs for maintenance and operation of the chosen workplace. Money spent in these areas may have a high payback, but it still is money that can't be used for some other aspect of the organization's activities.

Another scarce resource is the time and attention of members: executives, facilities professionals, and employees in general. In a sense this is money, since people are paid for their time, but the cost goes beyond

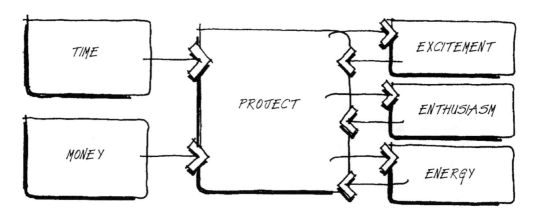

NONRENEWABLE RESOURCES   RENEWABLE RESOURCES

TIME AND MONEY ARE IMPORTANT NONRENEWABLE
RESOURCES, BUT TO SUCCEED OVER THE LONG TERM,
PROJECTS MUST NOURISH RENEWABLE HUMAN RESOURCES.

dollars. Attention given over to workplace design, management, and change is attention that is not being focused on other critical areas. In addition, real attention requires a psychological investment. A critical mass of familiarity and experience with the problem is necessary in order to make a useful contribution. In today's fast-paced, ever-changing work environment this investment is often a more significant block to an effective process than is the dollar cost per se. Key executives are particularly likely to be squeezed here because they face an endless array of issues that compete for their attention.

A second class of resource is not fixed-sum, but expandable and renewable. This is the interest and enthusiasm of members of the system. When people get excited about the possibilities in an area of activity, they bring more energy to the process and get more done for a given block of time and attention. There is often also a "contagion" effect, where the enthusiasm of a few stimulates the imagination of many. Rather than being expended, the energy level available on a project can actually be increased as it progresses. Conversely, if the process tends to give people a feeling that nothing exciting can happen and their efforts will make little difference, their enthusiasm and subsequent energy tend to evaporate quickly.

Limited Resources
Require Innovation

Working with limited economic resources can be seen as a block, but it can also operate as a challenge that helps to stimulate innovation. Obtaining maximum value from minimum expenditure necessitates doing things differently, not digging the same trench deeper. We recently asked an executive in a company that is about to build a new headquarters why the company was repeating a design that many employees felt was too closed and barrier-ridden, forming blocks to interdepartmental collaboration. The executive said, "The project team took this approach because they were concerned solely with fitting everyone into the floor space we have leased. It seemed easiest and most cost effective to use a whole array of closed offices like we have now." The only issue the team wanted to address was how to fit everyone into the given space at the least cost. The size of the space was chosen for financial reasons without much consideration given to how people would work in the space.

That project was an example of a factor we sometimes encounter when trying to promote thoughtful design: the assumption that when you have limited resources, you can't afford to do anything except repeat the current pattern of traditional offices and workspaces. A companion assumption is that if you go to a different (say, less closed) layout, you will have to reduce density and thereby increase costs. There is some truth to this if the approach is simply to substitute work stations for enclosed offices, but there are so many possible approaches that there is no reason this has to be the case. If leaders exercise creativity and flexibility in examining how space is actually used, they can often do more with less. We have already described such efforts (for instance, the free-address system, or the Cave and Commons approach) in the first section of this book.

Doing More with Less

If done thoughtfully, good places can be made for a full range of activities, without having to duplicate all-purpose spaces for everyone in residence. A small project team in a manufacturing firm did this using only existing furniture and the additions of laptop computers.

The team was led by a dynamic manager who was given the mission to create a new computerized order-entry process. He was told he could select a team that he felt could get the job done (in fact the team's motto is "Just Get It Done"). How he did this was his business. He could create whatever space and work pattern he wished, without being limited to the mainstream office culture. He was not, however, given unlimited resources. Everything had to be done in the area allocated to them within the existing building using the furniture that was available.

The result was a team office in which he and all the other professional and support staff, about fifteen people originally, sat in small open work stations that were the same size regardless of rank. The work stations were less than ninety square feet, about 30 percent smaller than the offices they were entitled to under existing company space standards.

These work stations surrounded a commons area with a conference table. One end of the area was given an informal atmosphere by furnishing it with unused sofas taken from elsewhere in the building. Privacy on the telephone was achieved by buying and refinishing an old wooden telephone booth (the only "new" furniture piece). The total amount of space occupied was considerably less than what the company space standards mandated for the group's size, yet the new configuration, supported by a manager who encouraged communication and teamwork, created a highly effective team and a group of motivated and energized staff doing more with less.

New was better here, but it was *new ways of using available resources*, not the purchase of new furniture or the expensive renovation of an existing space. The result was that this team, at a time when the morale of the rest of the company was quite low, was enthusiastic and upbeat. The team was willing to spend whatever time and energy it took to get the work done well and fast. The team's cohesiveness and commitment owed a lot to this manager's particular management style, and part of that talent was in understanding how to use the planning and design of the team's workplace to support the kind of teamwork he wanted. He exploited existing resources to create a high-performance workplace.

Matching Aspirations to Resources

One of the clearest tests of how well you are using your scarce resources is to examine them against what you are trying to accomplish. What is the match between the *level of aspiration* you have for a project and the *commitment of resources* you are able and willing to make to it?

For purposes of discussion, think of three simplified levels of aspiration:

Level I. A standard project; possibly more space but otherwise "business as usual."

Level II. An expansive, more elaborate departure from the current setting; possibly higher standards of furniture, finish, and amenities, and perhaps some simplification of the number of office sizes and a reduction in their sizes.

Level III. Intended innovation in types and uses of space; an experimental feel to the project, with organizational change implications.

For resource commitment, we use four conditions based on combining our two types of resources: size of budget (low versus high) and amount of leadership attention (low versus high). These combined produce four resource-commitment cases:

A. Low budget, low leadership attention

B. Low budget, high leadership attention

C. High budget, low leadership attention

D. High budget, high leadership attention

When we combine the levels of aspiration with the different levels of resource commitment, we get the twelve cases shown in the following table. In the cell for each combination we have described our prediction of the resulting flavor or feel of such a project. Since readers can scan the table for themselves, and generate other plausible predictions, we won't go into a detailed description of each cell here.

The main theme of the predictions is testing for a good match or a mismatch between aspirations and resources. Not surprisingly, there are likely to be better outcomes when the levels are matched than when they are not. For example, a Level I aspiration with low budget/low attention (a I-A project) is typically a good fit, with an emphasis on just getting the job done. In contrast, a Level III innovative project with low budget/low attention (III-A) is likely to be extremely frustrating for those charged with making it happen, and the outcomes are likely to fall far short of expectations.

Similarly, having high budget/high attention resources committed to a

Level of Resource Commitment

	A	B	C	D
LEVEL OF ASPIRATION FOR PROJECT	**LOW BUDGET LOW LEADER ATTENTION**	**LOW BUDGET HIGH LEADER ATTENTION**	**HIGH BUDGET LOW LEADER ATTENTION**	**HIGH BUDGET HIGH LEADER ATTENTION**
I Simple standard project; business as usual	Good match; just get the job done without too much fuss	Tradeoffs are important; focus on getting "most bang for the buck"	Overkill; easy project but potentially wastes money	Overkill; wastes time and money that could be used elsewhere
II Expansive, more elaborate new space; upgrade in furnishings and finish quality	Can't have it all; goals need to be scaled back	Poor fit, project team/facilities management people feel squeezed in spotlight	Probably a smooth process; can get good space; no change in organizational style	Smooth process; space probably tailored to leader's preferences
III Goals include changes in ways of working; innovation in space design and use	A real nonstarter; very frustrating to those involved in the project	Can't produce creative places at limited cost; some cost to innovation, especially in new design	New possibilities for space but not consistently in the same direction	Good match, wide range of potential outcomes with high impact on organizational functioning

Level I project (I-D) wastes resources, while the same resource commitment to a Level III change project (III-D) has the potential to go well and produce significant changes in work style and effectiveness.

Matching aspirations to resources should be one of the key criteria used when setting up a workplace planning process.

Pay Now or Pay Later

Creating new settings that really work requires taking the time and attention to analyze the assumptions that have shaped existing work patterns, as well as clarifying and then focusing hard on desired goals. This challenges the often unstated assumption underlying projects that recreate past settings; namely, that it is a waste of time and money to bother to do up-front diagnosis, analysis, goal setting, and process management when doing a new workplace. Budget-conscious project managers directed by their senior management to keep costs down assume that a tight project can't afford to spend resources on such "soft" activities.

This can be a classic case of being penny wise and pound foolish. The money and time spent on analysis, goal setting, concept clarification, and communication with the users get recouped in a faster and smoother design and building process. It also saves money by reducing the number of expensive building change orders made necessary by the failure to thoroughly understand occupant requirements in the design process.

Even more significantly, thoughtful beginnings lead to healthy work settings that promote good use of resources (time, energy, and running costs) throughout their useful life. Conversely, creating a bad pattern that incurs a lot of subsequent costs may end up being considerably more expensive than what would have been spent on the up-front work.

CHAPTER THIRTEEN

Making It Happen: Turning Workplace Vision into Reality

Creating workplaces that serve the organization well requires leaders who recognize the impact of work settings and policies on organizational health, question traditional assumptions about how to create and use work settings, and pay attention to issues of organizational ecology as a continuous part of their roles.

This final chapter summarizes a number of practical approaches and guidelines that experience suggests will tend to create a healthy pattern—that is, an effective and efficient organization that provides a high-quality, adaptive work environment for its members. We have grouped these principles, or rules of thumb, into four broad topics: aspects of work-setting design, processes for making and managing workplaces, dealing with organizational culture, and leadership roles in continuous learning.

Aspects of Work-Setting Design

- *Use visibility as a communications tool.* If you want people to know what is going on in the organization and who is doing what, create settings that make as much activity visible as possible. This may sound like a meaningless statement, or even circular, but it is definitely not the norm today.

Most layouts tend to wall off activities into neat compartments that bear no relation to each other, and therefore tend to have little effect on each other except when a special effort is made to "communicate."

We are suggesting that if space is deliberately designed to "display thinking" by making the daily activities of the organization more visible, communication among employees and awareness of what is going on in the organization will naturally increase, generating energy and interest throughout the firm. The other piece of this strategy is to encourage groups to show "work in progress" rather than letting information out only when they have finished something. When others see it in progress, they can provide much more interesting and helpful comments, if not always comfortable ones. Without this visibility, most reactions are after the fact, when they can't make much difference.

• *Use what you've got better*. In general, you can gain valuable resources by simply using better what you already have in your workplace. You need to be able to really see what you have, and the different

DISPLAYED THINKING KEEPS EVERYONE INFORMED

ways that it potentially can be used. This usually requires letting go of labels or names for places (the boardroom, the presentation room, and so forth) and seeing instead the qualities that they possess (a large space that can accommodate twenty people seated, good task lighting, a handy location next to the entry to the building).

You can accommodate a greater variety of activities simply by using current facilities in looser ways, with little or no out-of-pocket costs at all. The only cost is the energy required to look for attributes instead of labels, and to alter policies to allow such places to be used in unorthodox ways.

• *Locate facilities where people want to be.* If you are choosing a location for a startup company or for a new facility for an existing one, try to put it in a location that is attractive to the people who will work there. Again this sounds so obvious as not to be worth mentioning, and yet it is violated more times than it is followed. As long as companies have been created, leaders have tended to physically locate them in spots that make economic or logistical sense but not necessarily social-system sense.

This is changing today, as many new companies locate in highly attractive areas of the country such as the foothills of the Rockies, and in places such as North Carolina and Texas where the sun not only shines but housing is affordable. With today's electronic communications tools, physical location has become much less of a constraint for a knowledge-based company than it once was. Even for manufacturing operations, leaders are finding that locating them in attractive spots puts them ahead of the game in terms of recruiting high-quality staff.

• *Build for function, not form or image.* By simplifying or eliminating status as a determinant of workplace form, you can create settings that truly support what the users are trying to accomplish and be free to change it when needs have changed. The same holds for building to express a particular image of the system or its occupants—it's too rigid and costly in terms of inertia. Create the best place for what you do, and trust that this will be a positive image. If it's not, change what you do.

• *Build for change and expect to change it.* As much as possible try to create loose-fit settings, those that are not rigidly constructed for only one use in one style. The world will not stand still, and organizations that do will tend to drop out.

- *Build in some slack for spontaneity.* Just as it's hard to predict changes in work style or tasks ahead of time, it's hard to predict the spur-of-the-moment needs that people will have for work settings. Unless you *never* have any need for spontaneous activities such as meetings, don't build facilities that are so lean and efficient that there is no place for any activity that wasn't already programmed into them. Reduce the inertia cost of people putting off a good idea because there's no place to follow through on it.

- *Make some great places for informal contact during the workday.* Just as people need time by themselves, they also need to have high-quality interchanges with other people. In many organizations there are no good spots to do this, or if there are they tend to be in locations that make them unlikely to be used (too far off the beaten track, out of the way, in the way of traffic flow).

Every work setting should have a few very good interaction spots, such as small, cheery rooms with sofas, armchairs, coffee table, softer lighting, or whatever appeals to the people who will be using such spaces. If there is conscious attention to creating great interaction spots, that communicates a message to everyone that the leadership really values such exchanges and wants to encourage them. It also improves the quality of life for the users.

- *Speed up group development by giving teams a place.* As we have suggested several times in the book, workspace design can be a very effective tool in helping to create a sense of identity and teamwork in new groupings. In general, if you create a new, hybrid work entity or group, give it some concrete reality by also giving it a place of its own. This accomplishes a couple of things: it makes a clear commitment to the success of the new group; and it helps change the interaction patterns of the group, making it more likely that they will see and get to know one another and therefore begin to really think of themselves as a group. This should be done consistently as new groupings are created, so that it is expected and simply treated as part of business as usual.

- *Create a true center for a facility.* In a workplace that is a collection of individual and group spaces, work hard to create an inviting place near the actual center with good things that draw people—services, displays, entertainment, food and drink, and so forth—and make it the crossroads for coming and going through the system. This center will help provide the glue that holds the system together, by helping members be aware of the community as a whole, not just their own part.

• *Make a big deal out of having food and beverages available in central spots.* In our experience, having good food and drinks available in central spots is also a terrific community builder. Food draws people together just as it has throughout human history, and provides a kind of glue for the system. We have several clients who provide snacks such as fruit, bagels, donuts, and chips throughout the day, along with tea, coffee, soft drinks, and juices. Being generous with this sort of thing has big paybacks in terms of the climate that it helps to foster. People naturally feel a bit more relaxed when they are sharing something, and there is an almost festive quality to just being together in the café area.

• *Encourage workplaces that are more like home.* If you still have most people coming to the office, encourage them to add as many of the qualities of home as they would like it to have. This means having a variety of kinds of spaces, having artifacts that people like, and having spots for changes of pace and fun as well as for serious work. Sometimes these will in fact be the same spots used in different ways or by different people. We gave several examples of this in earlier chapters, and it may be one of the most important new directions. The point is to provide a rich setting that people feel at home in, so that they manage their time and pace to be both productive and creative over the long haul.

• *If you have people who travel a lot, create a great home base.* Many of today's service organizations (consulting firms, accountants, engineers, and the like) have a large percentage of professionals who work where the clients or customers are located, then come back to the firm to reconnect and do their own office work. Such return centers should be very carefully designed. They need to provide opportunities to relieve the stress of being "on stage" and on the road a lot. They also need to enhance connections with other people at the center. That suggests a mix of good personal work spots (not necessarily dedicated, though, as we have discussed earlier) and good mixing spots that allow people to see who's in the office and to talk to one another without the formality of appointments.

• *Pay special attention to entrances and exits.* Entrance design is very important in a work setting, since it shapes the first experiences people have when they enter it. Bad designs start people off on the wrong foot.

Similarly, an awkward or hard-to-find exit can leave a bad taste as the lasting impression one has of a place. Poor design of either makes people feel that the owners don't care about the experiences of visitors.

Processes for Making and Managing Workplaces

- *Get employees involved.* We have emphasized this throughout the book, and we'll do it one more time. The payoffs for involving users include better fit between the workplace and the users' needs, more excitement about the work, higher commitment to making the setting work, and better information about what fits and what needs changing. Designing the physical setting, when done right, is an invaluable form of organizational development.

- *Take care to do up-front direction setting.* As we have also stressed several times, workplace choices are much more effective when they are based on clear notions of the organization's mission, values, key challenges, expected growth patterns, future ways of working, and the like. Leaders must drive the processes of inquiry that will keep these current and keep them matched to facilities choices.

- *If you have strategic business units, let them control their workplaces.* The notion behind the strategic business unit (SBU) is to give the pieces of a larger organization the tools and freedom to do a job, then hold them accountable for their results. The principles of organizational ecology should be applied here as in other situations. Within budget parameters, the SBU leaders should be free to follow their own space strategy as part of managing their business for results. Controlling their space from the corporate facilities function sends a very contradictory message about whether they are really managing their business.

- *For space policies, just have a few good rules.* Members of SBUs or not, people in the organization should be as free as possible to use settings in ways that suit their needs, moods, and work styles. This suggests keeping overall facilities policies to a bare minimum, using only those that are essential to the overall direction you are trying to set. For example, a rule about coordinating space changes with adjacent groups helps maintain an integrated choice process, while lots of specific rules about what can or can't be changed tend to demoralize people. It turns them off to problem solving about the workplace, and they defer and treat it as someone else's problem.

• *Encourage and support local influence.* "Tinkering" is an activity that can keep workplaces relevant to current demands. It does it more efficiently than having all decisions driven and controlled by a central facilities function. Tinkering should be actively supported with information and resources, not merely tolerated.

• *Be wary of adding space as an automatic solution for feeling cramped.* Always test whether you feel you're out of space because there really are no places to accommodate new people or activities, or because the space you have is allocated too rigidly or unevenly. What are the actual occupancy levels of offices over the course of a day or week? Are the largest offices the least often occupied? Seek ways to use the same square footage more effectively. For instance, we have recently helped a couple of clients turn grand lobbies into activity centers for employees rather than sterile sitting areas waiting for the occasional visitor who needs somewhere to be for a few minutes (a very poor use of what is usually a very visible central spot in the organization).

As we have discussed in earlier chapters, there are a number of approaches to this way of thinking today: the free-address system, just-in-time scheduling, office "hoteling," and other forms of nonterritorial offices are aimed at better use of scarce space.

• *Establish a responsive change-management process.* For those changes to personal or group workspaces that do require professional or technical support, provide the resources to users in a timely manner, so they don't make do with inadequate facilities for long periods while waiting their turn. This also helps combat a climate of cynicism, which can develop if big delays are standard. People tend to give up on trying to get changes made, and just make do.

• *Integrate support services.* Encourage the various building support services—food service, mail, information technology, maintenance, security, and so on—to think of themselves as one team in providing a high-quality environment for the occupants. The focus then becomes customer satisfaction and organizational effectiveness rather than the smooth operation of each individual unit.

- *Create policies to seek gains, not avoid losses.* Space-use policies should be simple and encourage positive behavior patterns (teamwork, communication, adaptability) rather than being driven by a failsafe mentality of trying to avoid possible aberrations in place use. If you focus on the positives there will still be some misfires, but they will tend to be inconsequential and worthwhile as learning experiences.

- *Define the problem before jumping to solutions.* Carefully describe the situation and identify what doesn't work about it, plus what you would like to have happening instead. Then it is possible to look at alternative ways to achieve the goal. Don't state the problem with an implied solution ("our problem is that we need to have more space,"), but with what's missing, doesn't work, or needs to be done ("we need to be able to have forty new people work here within three months"). If you can stick to the problem, you are free to consider a range of alternatives (lease more space, have them work somewhere else, change the way workspaces are assigned, create new group work areas).

Dealing with Organizational Culture

- *Make conscious choices about the impact of culture when doing a facilities project.* Do a diagnosis of the current organizational culture when working on mission, values, key success factors, and project goals. Assess basic assumptions to test which ones need to be changed to match projected use of the new facility and which ones are unlikely to be changeable. The top leaders have to lead the way in being willing to openly test their cultural assumptions.

- *Change the culture through concrete experiences.* You can create events and experiences that can loosen up the traditional assumptions about how things have to work. For example, if no one will use the boardroom for meetings, even though it is intended to be available for such use, design a specific event to be held there, to get people comfortable with it, and follow with a clear message from the top that it is intended to be used as a resource for meetings but is currently underutilized.

- *Promote a more inclusive definition of "real work" in the system.* Help people accept and value the whole range of activities that can be used to accomplish tasks, get new ideas, and solve problems: writing, thinking, talking to others, moving around, staring into space, eating, drinking, and so on. Anything can be useful in the right moment, and trust should be placed in the members to be able to decide what they should do next (including taking time out to regenerate their energy).

Leadership Roles and Continuous Learning

• *Work at developing explicit models of the different roles you should play in the management of your organization's settings.* There is no substitute for having thought about what you should get involved in and (just as important) what you should not. Get your role clear in your own mind and discuss it with others. Share expectations for your and others' roles, and negotiate them periodically so that others know what they should be doing and what they can expect from you.

• *Encourage feedback from a variety of sources and levels about how well the workplace is supporting your organization and its mission.* There is no substitute for feedback from occupants of different parts of the system, and you must beware of thinking that your own experience is representative of others. As a company president once told us, "I don't see why people feel that my office is cold and intimidating; it's a very homey place." And it was—to him, since it was his home. Others saw it as imposing, hidden away, and threatening since their experiences there were of being chewed out by the president in one-way performance reviews. If you create conditions where people will tell you how they see the place working, you'll be surprised at some of what you hear.

One way to maintain this feedback is to create some sort of sounding board that cuts across functional, operational, and hierarchical lines to give you a cross-section of experiences. It also helps to involve people who are really interested in the area of workplace design and impact.

• *Look for articles, videos, and other forms of information that will help you learn more about organizational ecology and its impact on your organization.* The more you take in new ideas and trends in the field, the more useful questions that will raise about how your own places might be improved. Not all experiments will represent ideas you should try yourself, but they will raise interesting questions about what the people were trying to do and the new options they perceived for how to do it. Also look at architecture, interior design, and house magazines occasionally, just to get a feel for the new ideas in the field of space design. It's good to read outside your field of expertise anyway, as a means to making new connections and keeping loose about your assumptions about the world today.

• *Get out and look at examples of what has been done with space in other organizations.* Take the trouble to visit other organizations you have heard are doing something interesting with their workplace. Look at what they have done, and talk with those who did it about how they did it and what they were trying to accomplish. Take other people with you so that you are building a cadre of people who think about alternative workplace strategies in a looser way. To this end, you can also hire consultants to do workshops on organizational ecology and trends in design and management of settings.

Look at settings other than offices, too: public spaces, trade shows, expositions, museums (which often devote tremendous attention to detail and desired effect in their layout), and so on.

• *Get out and explore areas in your own organization.* Go see for yourself what different workplaces are like in your system, and talk to the people there about what work life is like for them. You never know what you will see and hear unless you take the trouble to do this periodically. We guarantee there will be surprises: conditions you wouldn't wish on anyone; areas where great things have been done with few resources and no fanfare—which could be applied around the system.

Getting around is good for your health, helps you to connect with others in the organization, and generates new ideas that can be followed up from your own vantage point. It also sends a message about your general interest and concern for people's working conditions.

• *Manage organizational ecology by doing a good job in the basic role of organizational leader.* Lastly, there are the basic leadership roles discussed earlier that are vital to developing and maintaining an effective workplace. These include:

• Keeping the vision, values, and mission of the system in focus, and testing for agreement.

- Identifying change goals for business, culture, structure, and the like.

- Setting overall standards for measuring the health of the organization.

- Structuring data-collection processes for monitoring all of the above.

- Structuring a workplace management process, including change management and the running of major projects; structuring ways to involve others in the process.

- Modeling effective use of workplaces in your own behaviors, so that you set a tone of thoughtfulness and conscious choice making.

In Closing: Creating New Places Versus Renovating Existing Facilities

For our final discussion, we would like to consider a recurring issue that contains many of the issues of organizational ecology, in terms of both content and process. To produce a better match between desired ways of working and the organization's work settings, is it necessary to build a completely new place?

We have a bias toward creative reuse of existing facilities if this is at all feasible. Even when there is considerable dissatisfaction with the current facility, there is a kind of embedded energy in the place that is lost if it is simply abandoned. In many cases the perceived constraints are caused by the assumptions that are made about how space can be shaped, allocated, and used, rather than by inherent properties of the setting itself. If a diagnosis suggests that this is indeed the case, you may be able to free up the work possibilities by changing standards, policies, and other constraints on use, rather than throwing time and money into a new project. In fact, new projects often don't solve the problem anyway, because basic assumptions about how work is done and space is used have not changed.

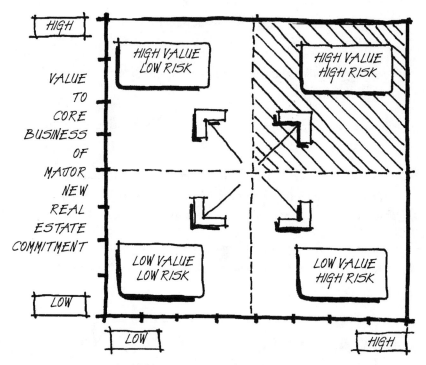

UNCERTAINTY ABOUT FUTURE NEEDS

WHEN DOES IT MAKE SENSE TO RISK A MAJOR CAPITAL EXPENDITURE?

Our rule of thumb here is simple: be very wary of getting into large-scale new projects unless they are absolutely necessary, such as when the existing setting is so confining or constraining that it will not be possible to function there in the ways that are needed for the future health of the organization.

The other key factor to consider is the accelerated rate of change in the environment of most organizations today. Driven by increasing uncertainty about markets, competitors, government regulations, environmental impact issues, technological advances, and the like, this turbulence makes it difficult to create brand-new work settings that are sized and equipped for the next change. In some cases, new facilities are obsolete before they are occupied, and in others it's even hard to know whether the place will be needed at all. Conceptions of what a corporate "headquarters" is are changing, and there are those who say that as a physical entity it may no longer be very useful in many enterprises.

All of this suggests to us that this is a time to be conservative about investing in major new office facilities, and progressive about experimenting with ways to use the facilities you already have. This not only saves potentially unnecessary investments, it takes advantage of the symbolic effects of working in a setting that has embedded in it the history of the enterprise and its people.

Having said this, we must also admit that analysis will sometimes show that the current setting just cannot support the level or variety of activities needed in the future. The flip side of the symbolic messages in the current setting is that if you want to truly change the culture and the way that people work, you may be fighting too much of an uphill battle to do it in the old setting. In some cultures the boardroom will always be the boardroom, a shrine to history and hierarchy, and you have to create an entirely new space if you want people to use it in different ways.

Between a renovation and creating a totally new place, there are obviously a number of other options. As a general strategy, we feel that it is best to first ask questions about policies and use patterns when sensing the need for workplace improvement, simply because these can be changed without a major capital expense. When you do choose to do some sort of renovations, they should occur in the context of a relatively continuous process of space management, rather than only when there is an unavoidable space crisis.

As we have described throughout this book, you are ahead of the game if you have regularly gathered information about basic questions such as:

- What are we trying to do here?

- How is this changing and how quickly?

- What aspects of the setting are hindering us in changing?

- Are we making assumptions that are limiting the ways we are using our work settings?

- What alterations do we need to make to fit our changing needs, which will gain us the most flexibility for the money and time involved?

The point is to be assessing the match between settings and ways of working as you go along, so that changes become less abrupt and more part of business as usual. It is also important that this assessment include data from a range of types of users, so that the answers are not projections of what things look like from the top of the system.

As we have also discussed earlier, many of the physical changes that would be useful are low-cost interventions—rearranging some work stations, improving lighting, hanging some graphics in strategic spots, painting dingy hallways or stairwells so they don't feel so demoralizing, giving a group more latitude to rearrange common workspaces and include team-type furniture, and so on.

If you have good notions about how ways of working need to change, these will have a big return for a modest investment. If you don't have such concepts, spending major dollars on a totally new work setting carries the risk of not making very much practical difference in the long run. Being creative about organizational ecology doesn't necessarily require a large budget, but it does require a regular investment of time and attention in checking how you're doing and setting updated goals about how you want the members of the organization to be able to work.

References

Allen, T. *Managing the Flow of Technology.* Cambridge, Mass.: MIT Press, 1977.

Barker, R. G., and Gump, P. V. *Big School, Small School.* Palo Alto, Calif.: Stanford University Press, 1964.

Becker, F. "Form Follows Process at Dynamic Lloyds of London." *Facilities Design and Management,* Feb. 1988, pp. 54–58.

Becker, F. *The Total Workplace: Facilities Management and the Elastic Organization.* New York: Van Nostrand Reinhold, 1990.

Becker, F. "Adding Value Through Process Management." *Industrial Development,* Dec. 1993, pp. 1395–99.

Becker, F., Davis, B., and Sims, W. *Managing Space Efficiently.* Ithaca, N.Y.: Cornell University International Workplace Studies Program, 1990.

Becker, F., Quinn, K. L., Rappaport, A. J., and Sims, W. R. *New Working Practices: Benchmarking Flexible Scheduling, Staffing and Work Location in an International Context.* Ithaca, N.Y.: Cornell University International Workplace Studies Program, 1993.

Becker, F., Quinn, K. L., Rappaport, A. J., and Sims, W. R. *Implementing Innovative Workplaces.* Ithaca, N.Y.: Cornell University International Workplace Studies Program, 1994.

Becker, F., Rappaport, A. J., Quinn, K. L., and Sims, W. R. *Telework Centers: An Evaluation of the North American and Japanese Experience.* Ithaca, N.Y.: Cornell University International Workplace Studies Program, 1993.

Breckenfield, G. "The Odyssey of Levi Strauss." *Fortune,* March 22, 1982, pp. 110, 112.

Brinkerhoff, R. O., and Dressler, D. E. *Productivity Measurement: A Guide for Managers and Evaluators.* New York: Sage Publications, 1990.

Finlay, S. K. *Benefits, Costs, and Policy Strategies for Telecommuting in Greater Vancouver.* Unpublished Master's of Business Administration thesis, Simon Fraser University, Vancouver, Canada, 1991.

Froggatt, C. *The Effect of Corporate Space and Furnishings Policies on Employee Workspace and Policy Satisfaction.* Master's thesis, Cornell University, Ithaca, New York, 1985.

Goffman, E. *The Presentation of Self In Everyday Life.* New York: Doubleday and Company, 1959.

Hall, E. T. *The Silent Language.* New York: Fawcett World Library, 1959.

Joroff, M., and Becker, F. *Innovations in the Workplace: Process To Achieve Change.* Atlanta, Ga.: Industrial Development Research Foundation CRE 2000 Workplace Bulletin, 1994.

Joroff, M., Louargand, M., Lamert, S., and Becker, F. *Strategic Management of the Fifth Resource: Corporate Real Estate.* Atlanta, Ga.: Industrial Development Research Council, 1993.

Miller, T. *Telecommuting in Large Corporations.* New York: LINK Resources, 1992.

Pratt, J. H. *Myths and Realities of Working at Home: Characteristics of Home-Based Business Owners and Telecommuters.* Austin, Tex.: Joanne Pratt Associates, 1993.

Quaid, M., and Lagerberg, B. *Puget Sound Telecommuting Demonstration, Executive Summary.* Olympia, Wash.: Washington State Energy Office, 1992.

Rheingold, H. *The Virtual Community: Homesteading on the Electronic Frontier.* Reading, Mass.: Addison-Wesley, 1993.

Romei, L. K. "Telecommuting: A Workstyle Revolution?" *Modern Office Technology*, May 1992, p. 38.

Spinks, W. A. "Satellite and Resort Offices in Japan." *Transportation*, 1991, pp. 343–63.

Weiner, E. "The Transportation Implications of Telecommuting." *Proceedings of Telecommute '93*, Washington D.C., Oct. 19–21, 1993.

Whitehall, H. (ed.) *Webster's New Twentieth Century Dictionary of the English Language Unabridged.* New York: World Publishing Company, 1951.

Further Readings

Becker, F. *The Total Workplace: Facilities Management and the Elastic Organization*. New York: Van Nostrand Reinhold, 1990.

Boyett, J. H., and Conn, H. P. *Workplace 2000: The Revolution Reshaping American Business*. New York: Dutton Press, 1991.

Davidow, W. H., and Malone, M. S. *The Virtual Corporation: Lessons from the World's Most Advanced Companies*. New York: HarperCollins, 1992.

Doeringer, P. B. (ed.) *Turbulence in the American Workplace*. New York: Oxford University Press, 1991.

Duffy, F. *The Changing Workplace*. London: Phaidon Press, 1992.

Gray, M., Hodson, N., and Gordon, G. *Teleworking Explained*. New York: Wiley, 1993.

Hammer, M., and Champy, J. *Re-engineering the Corporation*. New York: HarperCollins, 1993.

Handy, C. *The Age of Paradox*. Cambridge. Mass.: Harvard Business School Press, 1994.

Johansen, R. *Groupware: Computer Support for Business Teams*. New York: Free Press, 1988.

Olmsted, B., and Smith, S. *Creating a Flexible Workplace: How to Select and Manage Alternative Work Options*. New York: AMACOM, 1989.

Schrage, M. *Shared Minds: The New Technologies of Collaboration.* New York: Random House, 1990.

Steele, F. *Making and Managing High-Quality Workplaces: An Organizational Ecology.* New York: Teachers College Press, 1986.

Steele, F. *The Sense of Place.* New York: Van Nostrand Reinhold, 1981.

Index

and costs, 18; and criteria of
organizational health, 21–26;
reframing debate for, 18–19. *See
also* Performance assessment
Programming phase, 162
Promotion, for teleworkers, 105,
112

Q

Quaid, M., 111
Quality: defining workplace,
191–193; and measuring productivity, 19–20; retaining history
for, 194
Quinn, K. L., 48, 110n, 116n, 120n,
133, 155

R

Rappaport, A. J., 48, 110n, 116n,
120n, 133, 155
Real estate, loose-fit approach to,
56–58
Reality testing, in workplace, 22–23
Renovation, versus new
facilities, 213–216
Resources: limited, 198; matching
aspirations to, 200–202; for orga-
nizational ecology, 196–197; for
planning, 202; using available,
198–199. *See also* Spending
Reward systems, and measuring
productivity, 20
Rheingold, H., 114
Rodgers, C., 61
Rogers, C., 31
Roine, P., 172
Romei, L. K., 105

S

Safety, for workers, 86–88, 92–93
Scandinavian Airline Systems (SAS),
7, 81, 182–183
Service facilities: fixed spine for,
54–55; integrating, 209; shared,
80–81. *See also* Magnet centers
Sick-building syndrome, 90–91

Signage, in workplace, 43, 44
"Silent language," 29, 38–42
Sims, W. R., 48, 110n, 116n, 120n,
133, 155, 166, 191, 192
Size, and real estate, 56–58
Société Générale, 194
SOL, 147; business-driven
approach of, 125–132
Sony building, 15–16
Space: policies for, 208–209, 210;
solutions to cramped, 209; stan-
dards for, 174–175; as status, 24,
27–28, 33–38
Spending: and quality, 191–193; sat-
isfaction with results of, 196. *See
also* Resources
Spinks, W. A., 111
Sprint, 147
Status, space as, 24, 27–28, 33–38
Steelcase, Inc., 99, 100, 174;
Corporate Development Center
of, 71–77
Steiner, R., 16
Strategic business unit (SBU), 208
Support services: fixed spine for,
54–55; integrating, 209; shared,
79–81. *See also* Magnet centers

T

Tandem, 116
Task accomplishment, 23
Taylor, F., 16
Teamwork: communication
for, 69, 70–71; Hexcel's design
for, 64–67; and organizational
culture, 84–85; in planning, 155;
and "real work," 67–69;
Steelcase's design for, 70–77; suggestions for increasing, 83–84;
and workplace environment, 40
Technology: in business-driven
nonterritorial office, 130; information, 51–52, 57, 111, 146–147;
for virtual office, 113–114
Telecommuting. *See* Telework
Telework: home-based, 104–109;